Pneumatikos

by Ron Crawford

PNEUMATIKOS PUBLISHING
P.O. 595351
Dallas, TX 75359

info@pneumatikos.com

© 2002 by Ron Crawford

Published by Pneumatikos Publishing
P.O. Box 593531
Dallas, TX 75359
E-Mail: info@pneumatikos.com
www.pneumatikos.com

First printing, September, 2002

Printed in the United States of America. All rights reserved under International Copyright Law. No part of this publication may be reproduced, stored in a retrieval system or transmitted in any form or by any means--for example, electronic, photocopy, recording—without the prior written permission of the publisher. The only exception is brief quotations for printed reviews.

ISBN #0-9720681-3-9

Morris Publishing
3212 E. Hwy 30
Kearney, NE 68847

Cover Art Work by Fabian Arroyo

Unless otherwise noted, Scripture quotations are from the HOLY BIBLE, Authorized King James Version.

Table of Contents

Introduction	1
1 – PNEUMATIKOS: The Spiritual Ones	7
2 – The Covenant With The Earth	23
3 – The Order of Melchizedek	33
4 – To Be Or Not To Be	49
5 – How Pneumatikos Develops	59
6 – Pneumatikos Ministry Within the Church	71
7 – Worshipful Warriors	89
8 – Creative Worship of the Pneumatikos	97
9 – Pneumatikos Blessings In The Heavenlies	115
10 – Pneumatikos Wickedness In High Places	129
11 – On Earth As It Is In Heaven	145
12 – The King Is Coming	163
13 – Fear Not	177

Preface

If you are starting to read this book and have not yet read **The Saints** by Ronald Crawford, please take the time to read it first. **Pneumatikos** is the second volume in a series. It continues to unfold tremendous revelations of what God has in store for His church in these last days.

Pastor Crawford is a long time student of the Word. To this firm foundation, God has added an incredible anointing for receiving revelation from the heart of the Father that is fresh and alive. These revelations are insights from the Lord that bring greater understanding to many scriptures that have been ignored by most students of the Word. One of the tenets of our faith is an unshakable belief in the Holy Spirit inspiration of every single word of scripture and that every word is applicable for today.

The number of revelations he is receiving is beyond anything I have ever witnessed. Those that are familiar with the ministry of Watchman Nee will recognize that Nee had this type of anointing as well. Nee believed that every true minister of the Word must spend so much time with the Father that a fresh revelation from God's living Word comes forth every time they teach or preach. The ministry of Pastor Crawford is one of serving fresh manna at every spiritual meal.

The revelations within these pages have incredible ramifications for the Body of Christ. God intends to have a core of people from within the general church who are going to battle the enemies of righteousness in the last days. I challenge you to read both of these books and weigh the validity of this message for the church. Then ask yourself if you are willing to make a greater commitment to serving the Lord. The enemies of righteousness are opposed to those in right standing with the Lord and completely aligned with His perfect purposes. To walk in the purposes of God requires a totally dedicated believer, which is not the type of believer that makes up most of the church today.

God is looking for those who will worship Him in spirit and in truth. We must become more spiritual if we are to be transformed by God. Those who have an undying passion for the heart of the Father and will allow Him to fashion and transform them will become "spiritual ones," called in the Greek, **<u>Pneumatikos</u>**.

Paul David Harrison

Introduction

> Proclaim ye this among the Gentiles; Prepare war, wake up the mighty men, let all the men of war draw near; let them come up:
>
> Joel 3:9

Perhaps there is no finer scriptural mandate for this book than the one cited by the prophet Joel. God is calling to the mighty men of David to come forth for battle.

The church has enjoyed a period of relative ease in which it has become expert at cultivating and refining its methods and fields of service. God now issues a clarion call to take those "abiding" implements and turn them into weapons of battle.

God has been preparing mighty men for some time. These men and women of the Most High are in the process of receiving unique training for the coming day of combat. The pending conflict has much at stake and will ensure the fate of the entire planet.

On the opposing side are dark princes of the enemy kingdom commanded by Lucifer. Their time is short, and they will fight with every ounce of determination and villainy within them. The conflict between the forces of righteousness and the kingdom of darkness will rock the world. Much of humankind will be killed and a significant portion of the planet destroyed. War has already been prepared. It is now time for the mighty men to be awakened.

The initial mobilization will involve incredible signs and wonders from the Lord. Angelic visitation will be a regular facet of daily existence. Entire neighborhoods will become zones of God's visitation. The glory of the Lord will be revealed, and all flesh will see it together. Little children will declare the prophetic voice of God, and the hand of the Lord will enforce the words. Creative miracles will be common occurrences. The dead will be raised. These miraculous demonstrations will be witnessed by entire cities.

Saints will move forth in unparalleled dominion and confidence. Entire nations will return to righteousness, and the name of Jesus will be proclaimed in palaces from one continent to another. As these saints move forth in power, the light of heaven will be visibly depicted upon their clothing, just as it did upon the raiment of Moses and Jesus.

The battle for righteousness is here. God is recruiting those with whom He can entrust His power and presence. They will fulfill a priestly office before Him, and their Chief is none other than the Lord Jesus Christ.

The Word of God speaks very openly of these people. They are personified in passages throughout the New Testament, but their identity has been hidden under the hand of God until this hour of revelation. The New Testament entitles these champions the **spiritual** ones, or the ***Pneumatikos***.

As you read this book, allow the Lord to guide you in an examination of the truths. Know that the enemy does not want you to glean this message. Religious tradition, in alliance with the spirit of religion, will attempt to convince you that this teaching is unscriptural and invalid. Bear in mind that every move of God has initially been greeted in this way.

These saints are identified as a royal priesthood that flow out from a **spiritual** house, which is defined by the Greek word ***pneumatikos***. Saints will comprise *pneumatikos* and flow out from this priestly house. Within the Old Testament, God speaks of a differentiation between saints and priests. In one passage these priests are notated as being excellent ones. Priests and excellent ones are notable definitions of what *pneumatikos* is to be within the church.

> **2 Chronicles. 6:41** Now therefore arise, O Lord God, into thy resting place, thou, and the ark of thy strength: let thy priests, O Lord God, be

clothed with salvation, and let thy saints rejoice in goodness.

Psalm 16:3 But to the saints that are in the earth, and to the excellent, in whom is all my delight.

Psalm 132:16-18 I will also clothe her priests with salvation: and her saints shall shout aloud for joy. 17 There will I make the horn of David to bud: I have ordained a lamp for mine anointed. 18 His enemies will I clothe with shame: but upon himself shall his crown flourish.

In the New Testament, the saints are distinguished from the general church, the prophets and the martyrs. Although saints will populate and demonstrate the characteristics of all three of these groups, they are clearly established as also being something different. It is vital that the reader obtain a copy of the companion volume to this writing which is entitled **The Saints**.

The study of the ***pneumatikos*** is both instructive and compelling. The purpose of this book is to provide clarity of understanding regarding this remarkable group. Power and insight will be released into the church through this group of people and will also be administrated by them.

Prepare yourself for a look at what is to come. During the course of the next several years, the information contained within this book will seem commonplace as the wonders of the Lord will be known within the mainstream of the cultures of the earth. For this hour, may this writing serve as a voice crying, "Prepare, for the Lord is coming. Wake up the mighty men!"

Pneumatikos

chapter 1

PNEUMATIKOS: The Spiritual Ones

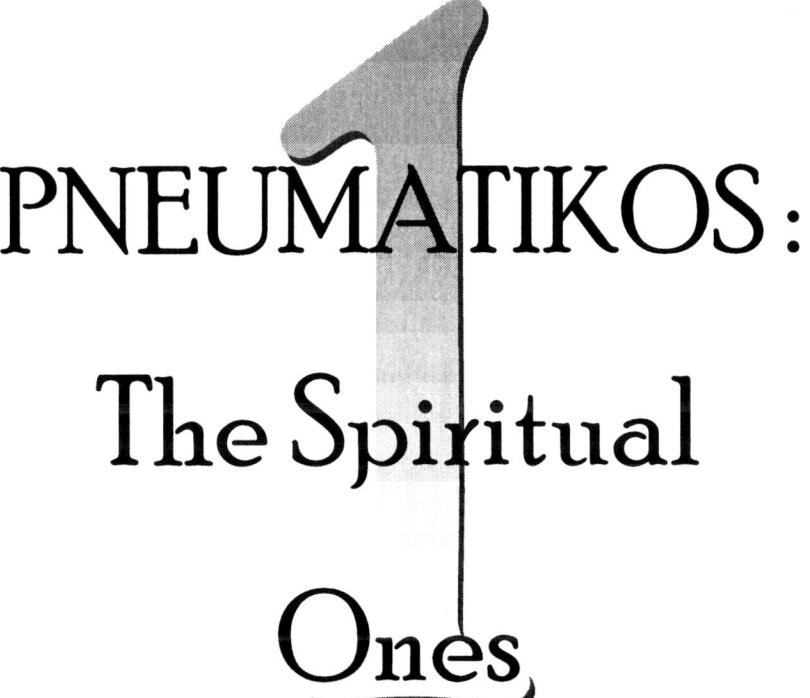

> **1 Peter 2:4-5** To whom coming, as unto a living stone, disallowed indeed of men, but chosen of God, and precious, 5 Ye also, as lively stones, are built up a spiritual house, an holy priesthood, to offer up spiritual sacrifices, acceptable to God by Jesus Christ.

How many times have we read this passage and assumed that the **spiritual** were simply those that were holier than everyone else? Usually, it is a far stretch of the imagination to believe that this passage might actually be talking about us.

As a matter of fact, we probably did not want to associate with the holy ones very much because most of them were somewhat odd in behavior or abrasive in their scope of ministry. In the modern church there has been little interest in being different for the cause of Christ. Therefore, anything that is "out of the ordinary" is generally brought into rapid alignment with the status quo. Those that display an aberration from that pattern are generally labeled "holy" or extreme.

What a far cry from the original plan of God. It seems in the reading of the Word, most of God's true friends were peculiar. They fit into the category of being odd or at the very least, different. Our aversion to the unusual is undoubtedly a trait of societal influence. Nobody wants to be perceived as being abnormal on a personal or corporate level. We want to be appealing, and a watchword for the church today is "seeker friendly." This common phrase is a euphemism for attracting as many people as possible by any means possible. In the process it would be terrific if these newcomers found God in some manner.

The Bible paints a totally different landscape for the composition of the church. We should love one another but be perceived as fools for Christ's sake. As a Pentecostal from a very young age, I can remember when it meant something distinctive to be filled with the Spirit. Not only did we listen to historical accounts of those that suffered because of their desire to be filled by the Spirit of God with the evidence of speaking in tongues, but we also felt that there was a difference between us and everyone else. Jesus was our savior, but He had also filled us with the Holy Ghost. This made our experience with God a singular issue, and we did not even think of trying to be otherwise.

Today you can attend a cross-sampling of "Christian" churches and not find a real difference between any of them. To say that your church is "Spirit filled" does not necessarily mean that you desire for the Spirit of God to do whatever He would like to do in your worship services.

Even within the churches that are wholeheartedly trying to follow after God, there is pressure to conform. The conforming influence can take place through internal and external sources. Internally, the thought process of the church itself will encounter contesting, just as the mind will protest the movements of the spirit of a person, so the mindset of the local body will either submit or resist what God is doing. Externally, the intimidation of competition with other movements or churches can cause a roadblock on the path to obedience to God. Pride definitely is a fuel for both of these hindrances.

In essence, the believer and the church need to be more spirit minded than earthly minded. God is Spirit, and so is man. Humans were created in the very image of God, but we live our lives as if the earth were their entire existance. The church at Pentecost was infused with the wind of God, but we live as though our first breath after birth was all the breathing that we would ever need.

We must become a people that flow in the breath of God. Our purpose as created beings is to focus upon the things pertaining to God's Spirit as opposed to the machinations of man's best thought. God has created and called us to serve Him as a people that are spiritual. Spiritual people are literally those that breathe the wind of God and are moved about by His wind.

THE SPIRITUAL ONES

To describe these spiritual ones the New Testament uses the Greek word *pneumatikos*, which means "establishment of the spirit, wind or breath." *Pneumatikos* is used only twenty-three times in the New Testament and is usually translated as **spiritual** in the King James Version. As we examine each instance of the word within the New Testament, a unique picture of *pneumatikos* unfolds before our eyes. The *pneumatikos* is a vital organ within the New Testament church that we need to rediscover and implement today.

SPIRITUAL HOUSE

> **1 Peter 2:5** Ye also, as lively stones, are built up a spiritual house, an holy priesthood, to offer up spiritual sacrifices, acceptable to God by Jesus Christ

Pneumatikos is utilized in this passage to depict its fundamental basis; that being a household of priests. This priesthood offers up specific sacrifices of prophetic and strategic importance. Quite literally, the *pneumatikos* establishes our seat of commune with the Lord in the heavenlies.

The priesthood denotes administration of responsibility before the very presence of God involving an absolute commitment to holiness. God will speak dynamically through this group concerning His ways and will use them to inspire a devotion to the holy. The ***pneumatikos*** house is established to offer up ***pneumatikos*** sacrifices acceptable to the Father by Jesus Christ.

The holy priesthood, representing the entire saintly flow, is comprised of the men and women that have devoted themselves entirely to God. What they offer to Him in the manner of sacrifice has nothing to do with their salvation as Christ Jesus has already provided that atoning work. These sacrifices are ordained of God to minister to Him in the implementing of His ways. In the Old Testament there were many types of offerings that were yielded to God in order that the people of God could walk righteously before Him.

These sacrifices are said to be acceptable by Christ Jesus. This simply means that as our great forerunner, Jesus has patterned such sacrifice before God. He continually offered Himself so that the way of righteousness might be opened to those who would believe and accept Him. In like manner, the **spiritual** sacrifices of the ***pneumatikos*** will be offered.

The author of this passage of scripture was the Apostle Peter. Of all of the disciples, Peter was chosen to demonstrate the meaning of a relationship with the Heavenly Father. However, due to his brash demeanor, he was the least likely choice for this assignment. No matter what your personal obstacle, you can also find your place in the Father.

Jesus told Peter that the church would be built upon the foundational rock of relationship with the Father. Success does not depend upon your energies or skill, but on your pursuit of knowing the Heavenly Father. Look at what Jesus says to Peter regarding this issue.

> **Matthew 16:17-19** And Jesus answered and said unto him, Blessed art thou, Simon Barjona: for flesh and blood hath not revealed it unto thee, but my Father which is in heaven. 18 And I say also unto thee, That thou art Peter, and upon this rock I will build my church; and the gates of hell shall not prevail against it. 19 And I will give unto thee the keys of the kingdom of heaven: and whatsoever thou shalt bind on earth shall be bound in heaven: and whatsoever thou shalt loose on earth shall be loosed in heaven.

Strategic information and authority will proceed from a place of complete reliance upon God. This is the basis of wisdom and direction for things spiritual and will keep the church moving forward in ways that are mighty through God. Jesus instructed

Peter that the church would be built by revelation from the Father that would both tear down strongholds and build the church. The priesthood of the believer is to be one of kingdom taking.

A ROYAL PRIESTHOOD

> **1 Peter 2:9** But ye are a chosen generation, a royal priesthood, an holy nation, a peculiar people; that ye should shew forth the praises of him who hath called you out of darkness into his marvellous light.

Peter uses a very different term to describe the royal priesthood from that offered in Verse 5 and groups it with "a chosen generation," "an holy nation," and "a peculiar people." Peter chooses the words holy, saintly and chosen in the same verse, and he can only be referring to those that the Bible classifies as saints. They are the choice ones of God's heritage, sent to accomplish magnificent tasks of obedience and service to the Father.

Peter is writing this letter to the Gentile church, which is the Tabernacle of David according to Amos 9:11. The word for "generation" is a word for "nationalities," and the Gentile church is comprised of people from all over the globe that have been called out by God. The Holy Spirit speaks of the Gentile church as a royal priesthood and a holy nation. These have been called from darkness into the light to "shew forth the praises" of the Lord. *Arete,* the Greek word that is translated as **praises,** is an obscure word that means maturity or virtue. Therefore, this group of people will demonstrate the maturity of the Lord as they become like Him.

A royal priesthood speaks of transacting royal business. The saints are chosen for the purpose of serving the Father in this manner. Moving forth as lively stones, they overtake kingdoms of darkness and establish the Kingdom of God by virtue of His fire within them.

Within the pages of the Book of Zechariah, we discover an Old Testament example of this powerful principle. God chose Jerusalem as His own property. He fashioned a champion and sent that man to confront the very forces of hell. Joshua was that man, and we behold an example of the type of heavenly deliberation that regularly occurs.

> **Zechariah 3:1** And he shewed me Joshua the high priest standing before the angel of the LORD, and Satan standing at his right hand to resist him. 2 And the LORD said unto Satan, The LORD rebuke thee, O Satan; even the LORD that hath chosen Jerusalem rebuke thee: is not this a brand plucked out of the fire.

From out of the midst of the fire of God, individuals are chosen to embark on strategic duties of the Lord's choosing. Those who flow from the ***pneumatikos*** will become royal priests on the earth and in the heavenlies. In Acts 13 the prophets and teachers at Antioch ministered before the Lord, and from this ministry Paul and Silas were sent forth as apostolic messengers. These leaders at Antioch offered up royal or saintly sacrifices of righteousness in order that God's timely purpose for the Gentiles might be released into the world.

ROYAL SACRIFICES OF RIGHTEOUSNESS

Let us observe the distinct instances where this designation is used in scripture.

- **A Heart of Sacrifice**

   Psalm 51:16-19 For thou desirest not sacrifice; else would I give it: thou delightest not in burnt offering.17 The sacrifices of God are a broken spirit: a broken and a contrite heart, O God, thou wilt not despise. 18 Do good in thy good pleasure unto Zion: build thou the walls of Jerusalem. 19 Then shalt thou be pleased with the sacrifices of righteousness, with burnt offering and whole burnt offering: then shall they offer bullocks upon thine altar.

David speaks from the heart of one who pursued God with all of his might. This type of royal priesthood says that sacrifices of righteousness are those that flow from a heart that is contrite, or pulverized, into fine points of obedience. It is this type of relationship that comprises the *pneumatikos* and brings enhanced meaning to that which is detailed in the general *logos* of scripture.

- **A Mind of Sacrifice**

    Psalm 4:3-5 But know that the LORD hath set apart him that is godly for himself: the LORD will hear when I call unto him. 4 Stand in awe, and sin not: commune with your own heart upon your bed, and be still. Selah. 5 Offer the sacrifices of righteousness, and put your trust in the LORD.

As the royal priesthood commits to being broken before the Lord in devoted worship, the mind will become submitted to things **spiritual**. In this passage we discover that those that fill this role will wait patiently before the Lord in order to glean His directive.

- **A Body of Sacrifice**

    Deuteronomy 33:18-19 And of Zebulun he said, Rejoice, Zebulun, in thy going out; and, Issachar, in thy tents. 19 They shall call the people unto the mountain; there they shall offer sacrifices of righteousness: for they shall suck of the abundance of the seas, and of treasures hid in the sand.

Issachar was a tribe that was wise in the ways of the Lord. Zebulun was a valiant group of warriors that moved in harmony with precise directives of insight, and they regularly flowed as a mighty tandem in the land. It would seem that when God's directives are declared and carried out, the resultant obedience and victory is a sacrifice that is offered to God.

Zebulun represented the royal saints as mighty warriors that flowed forth from the wisdom of Issachar. Naphtali represented the general church that supports the ranks of the saints and *pneumatikos*. Interestingly, when Jesus came from John's baptism and subsequent wilderness temptation, He had to fulfill Isaiah's prophecy by going through the land of Zebulun and Naphtali. Jesus had already gleaned the mind of the Father (Issachar) and was stepping forth in timely fashion to effect obedience to that cause. He chose the prophetic path to depict the gathering of the saints and the general church.

PRIESTS AND KINGS

A *pneumatikos* priesthood establishes the framework for God to speak dynamically to, and on behalf of, His general church. From this powerfully impassioned atmosphere, a royal priesthood of saints proceeds to accomplish mighty deeds on behalf of the purpose of the Father.

Priests minister before God in the manner of His choosing. The entire order of saints enjoys this priestly ministry as they are continually accomplishing His bidding. A royal priesthood is a separate designation that must have a measure of rulership within. This structure of command is represented by kings.

> **Revelation 5:10** And hast made us unto our God kings and priests: and we shall reign on the earth.

One predominant theme emerges throughout the regions of the spirit realm, and that is the theme of authority. No angel, man, or enemy force will work outside of some type of authority structure. The saint will operate safely as he proceeds under the proper alignment of authority. Jesus patterned this lesson for us and continues to submit Himself to the authority of the Father.

Realistically, there are individuals that demonstrate His authority. Those that submit themselves to the bidding of the Master will be known as kings under God and will jurisdict His influence within their appointed structure. Initially, we might cringe at the thought of identifying a believer as a king. Many differing euphemisms come to mind, from generals to other titles of man's creation. God calls these people kings, and that is what they are before Him.

KINGS AND LORDS

> **Revelation 19:16** And he hath on his vesture and on his thigh a name written, KING OF KINGS, AND LORD OF LORDS.

Jesus appears in this passage as a triumphant warrior. His identity is clearly depicted by the title "KING OF KINGS and LORD OF LORDS." No other personage can make such a claim. He is the great God, but He also knows how to submit to the authority of the Father. He rules at the highest throne of all, but He also submits to that throne as He yields to the Heavenly Father. This is an incredible theme.

Many people know how to give commands, and there are those that understand how to obey. A few recognize what it means to do both. These are the servants of all who are the greatest of all. Jesus demonstrates this at the uppermost level. The God that is over all things is also the servant.

While this is an astounding lesson, there is also another magnificent thought found within this passage. The title of "KING OF KINGS and LORD OF LORDS" is located in two places on the Savior's clothing. By stating this on the vesture, we discover His identity and authority.

The breastplate will always classify our calling and influence. The labeling on the thigh addresses a carrying out of the mission as the legs characterize movement and acquisition. For an individual riding a horse, the thigh can communicate direction to the animal. This is a picture of authority and submission in every level.

LIVELY STONES

Those who minister before the Father in this framework in the heavens are people who quite literally walk in the heavens amidst the heavenly stones of fire. Lively stones are those that are ablaze, molten, and explosive. Stones begin moving and having life when they are molten like the lava that flows from a volcano. Closeness to the Heavenly Father and exposure to His fire causes people to become so pliable that they have the ability to establish and create new ground, to actually create things that were not there before, and to remove and/or set on fire what is already in existence. They become the embodiment of God's presence and purpose.

In this framework, a *pneumatikos* house is built where high-level **spiritual** issues regularly explode in the very midst as *pneumatikos* sacrifices that are called and ordained of the Holy Ghost are offered up to God. This level cannot be achieved by the striving of man but only through pressing into the Father, becoming His representatives and doing His bidding.

The New Testament has much to say regarding the existence and function of the *pneumatikos*. The **spiritual** ones will yield prophetic insight from the Father. This priesthood patterns itself following the priesthood of the Lord Jesus after the Order of Melchizedek. God's Word has much more to say about this facet of God's order.

chapter 2

The Covenant With The Earth

The earth is the Lord's and the fullness thereof. Those that study the written scriptures are familiar with these words, but few really believe that God means to claim the planet as His own. Within the heart of God, there is a jealousy for the land that belongs to Him. He intends to reclaim this place which was created to be a magnificent point of praise for Him. To do so, He is going to use those that are also created to praise Him.

When Adam was formed from the dust of the ground, God breathed His wind of life into the lifeless body of man. Adam was truly the first *pneumatikos*, created in the very form of God. God and man are both spirit beings, and Adam knew how to discern what God wanted and did not want. When Adam fell, mankind began to desire evil within that place of spiritual discernment, and God was forced to destroy mankind.

NOAH AND THE RAINBOW

When the population of the earth was eliminated during the great flood, God's grace delivered a man named Noah. He also gave Noah a sign of covenant for the earth. That covenant for the planet was in the shape of a beautiful rainbow.

Genesis 9:13 I do set my bow in the cloud, and it shall be for a token of a covenant between me and the earth.

This signature of God remains to this very day, and it is much more than a promise to spare the earth from watery destruction. It is a covenant for the planet, and Noah was given dominion. This bow was the signature of God, the first covenant with God upon the earth.

COLORS OF THE SIGNATURE OF GOD

Every rainbow that has ever been formed on this earth will follow the same pattern in its progression of seven colors. Each of these colors represents one of the seven winds of the Father. The progression of these colors depicts the sequence of how God conducts His business. Every *pneumatikos* individual needs to recognize that to flow in the patterns of God will guarantee victory upon the earth.

The first color to register in the rainbow is red, and it requires the least amount of lumens to register to the eye. From there, the model is always the same. The progression is consistently red, orange, yellow, green, blue, indigo blue and violet.

The world constantly uses this powerful expression from God in order to represent many causes, and many of them are anything but Godly. Curiously, the one color that is most often deleted from illustration of the rainbow is indigo blue, and this color most notably corresponds to the glory or person of God.

THE SEVEN SPIRITS OF GOD

The Bible tells us that God has seven spirits. These are depicted in the Book of Revelation, and it is imperative that we understand these dimensions of disclosure.

- **Winds**

    Revelation 1:4 John to the seven churches which are in Asia: Grace be unto you, and peace, from him which is, and which was, and which is to come; and from the seven Spirits which are before his throne;

These spirits, or winds, can also be defined as breath. God loves to speak, and whatever He does involves an audible expression. Our confession is essential for obedience to God's ways.

Trinitarians find it most convenient to simply honor the Lord by admitting to the existence of the Holy Ghost. Perhaps it would be most accurate for us to admit that the triune God has multiple facets within his *pneumatic* structure.

- **Lamps of Fire**

Revelation 4:5 And out of the throne proceeded lightnings and thunderings and voices: and there were seven lamps of fire burning before the throne, which are the seven Spirits of God.

A lamp produces light for direction and clarity. God's winds are mighty for the purpose of granting illumination of His paths and ways. Those that will look to understand God's ways must yield themselves to the winds of God.

Additionally, the lamps of God are depicted in the parable of the ten virgins. One might easily deduce that the wise virgins were ones that were apprised of the way that God's winds were moving according to His present truth. Those that will find themselves prepared in anticipation of the coming of the Lord will be familiar with the moving of the winds of the Spirit of God.

- **Eyes**

    Revelation 5:6 And I beheld, and, lo, in the midst of the throne and of the four beasts, and in the midst of the elders, stood a Lamb as it had been slain, having seven horns and seven eyes, which are the seven Spirits of God sent forth into all the earth.

The Bible speaks of the eyes of the Lord that search the earth looking for those that have a heart which will serve Him in obedience and devotion.

> **2 Chronicles 16:9** For the eyes of the Lord run to and fro throughout the whole earth, to shew himself strong in the behalf of them whose heart is perfect toward him.

Notice that the eyes, or winds of the Spirit of God, are searching for a perfected vessel. God will use this vessel to serve the current purposes of His Spirit. These perfected ones are committed to the righteousness of God. We find this connection established once again in the writing of David.

> **Psalm 34:15** The eyes of the Lord are upon the righteous, and his ears are open unto their cry.

It is apparent that the winds of the Spirit of God are continually moving upon creation. It is equally evident that this dimension of the person of God is regularly working with the righteous ones that are partnering with Him according to His will. This is an absolutely incredible reality.

IDENTIFYING THE SEVEN SPIRITS

Some will state that the seven spirits of God are concisely listed in Isaiah 11:2.

> **Isaiah 11:2** And the spirit of the Lord shall rest upon him, the spirit of wisdom and understanding, the spirit of counsel and might, the spirit of knowledge and of the fear of the Lord.

As powerful as this passage is, not all of the seven spirits are specifically listed therein. There are also other classifications of the Spirit of God listed throughout the Bible. Upon categorizing these scriptures and comparing them with colors that have been witnessed by seers in dreams, visions and active revelations, the Lord has blessed us with a defining meaning to associate color with wind.

Red	Judgment and Burning	Isaiah 4:4 ; 28:6
Orange	Grace and Supplication	Zechariah 12:10 Hebrews 10:29
Yellow	Wisdom and Revelation	Deuteronomy 34:9 Isaiah 11:2 Ephesians 1:17
Green	Prophecy and Supply Healing	Philippians 1:19 Revelation 19:10
Blue	Holiness	Romans 1:4
Indigo Blue	Glory of God	I Peter 4:14
Violet	Adoption and Truth	Romans 8: 2, 15 John 14:7 II Timothy 1:7

INTERPRETING THE WINDS

It is helpful to understand the pattern of God because it is the manner in which He operates. Let us consider the flow from both angles.

From heaven to earth: God begins by using someone who will affect His purposes upon the earth. A joint-heir, or king, will become intimately involved with the person of God. This individual will be entrusted with partnership status in accomplishing the purpose of God. This person is sent in saintly duty to accomplish holiness within the place of God's choosing. This individual will rely upon prophetic insights and apply wisdom and understanding to situations that are encountered. This application will engender grace and promotion into the place and to the people. The final point will be the applying of the plummet of righteousness into the place of judgment and burning. When these things occur, the glory of God will visit that place.

From earth to heaven: God visits the planet in His glory, which is predicated upon an intercessor that has paid the price of invitation and sacrifice. This visitation produces repentance from sin and a turning toward righteousness. As grace begins to grow, promotion and positive development begin to occur within the people and places of visitation. Insights into the ways of God will begin to become apparent, and prophetic perception will burst upon the scene. If these are accepted and acted upon, God will begin to entrust saintly duty and responsibility. As this is devotedly followed, God will reveal Himself in more intimate ways. In His timing, the very power and grandeur of His Kingdom will be shared and this individual will become a joint-heir and manifest the characteristics of being a friend of God. This is all so very simple and is God's prescription for the world. It is God's covenant for the earth as well as for the people who live upon it.

An understanding of these colors and patterns can be of great help to seers who are able to discern their presence. For instance, if a certain color were present, it would be safe to assume that God is moving in accordance with that signature upon the situation.

Also, if a color or colors are witnessed, the progression pattern can be traced in order to ascertain what might be coming next. If you perceive green and blue, you might become prepared for a dynamic visitation of the glory of God.

There are many possibilities of interpretation, and this is where the *pneumatikos* comes into play. They are called to cooperate with the winds of the Spirit of God. Discerning and judging what God desires to do will prepare a pathway for ready obedience. While extremely helpful in a ministry setting, we must remember that this rainbow was a covenant for the people and the land.

Noah was successful in building the ark but failed in his responsibility to have dominion in the earth. Many years passed before God offered his covenant again, and this time it was in the person of a man named Abram. God's covenant for the land and people were communicated in the mandate of righteousness. The episode in which it was conducted was one in which another of Noah's offspring functioned in the Spirit of God. That man's name was Melchizedek, and his order of ministry continues to this day.[1]

---

[1] For a further study obtain **Seer's Catalog** by Ron Crawford, Pneumatikos Publishing.

chapter 3

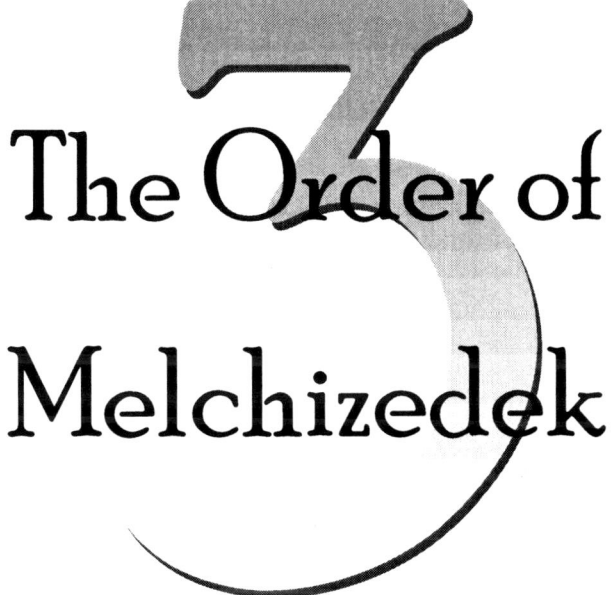

The Order of

Melchizedek

Melchizedek is one of the most intriguing characters in all of the Word of God. So little is known of him, and so much depends on what we do know. Abraham recognized this man as representing a priesthood unto the Most High, and our Lord Jesus affiliated His priesthood within this holy order.

This mysterious individual is spoken of in Genesis and in Hebrews and is firmly linked with everything that we are as a people of God. This king of peace, or king of righteousness, shows much of what we are to be in these end times.

> **Genesis 14:18-20** And Melchizedek king of Salem brought forth bread and wine: and he was the priest of the most high God. 19 And he blessed him, and said, Blessed be Abram of the most high God, possessor of heaven and earth: 20 And blessed be the most high God, which hath delivered thine enemies into thy hand. And he gave him tithes of all.

In acknowledging Melchizedek, Abram ordained the order of righteousness before the three groups of which he is the earthly father: the Jews, the Arabs and the Christians who walk in faith. The antichrist will undoubtedly appear as a priest after the Order of Melchizedek in an attempt to legitimize himself in the eyes of all three groups.

Melchizedek means the king of righteousness. On earth he was the King of Salem, which is the terrain that was to become

Jerusalem. Melchizedek came forth with the articles of communion after Abram had won a military engagement in which Lot was freed from the forces that kidnapped him and his family. Hebrews 7:3 declares that his order is without father and mother on earth, depicting the thought that his lineage of authority comes from the heavens.

The bringing of the elements of Holy Communion is significant. Many theologians define this as representing a type of Christ, but the main theme should not lead one to the impression that this man was actually Christ. Rather, the mandate of Christ for continued communion with God had to be established in the life of Abraham. Holy Communion speaks of the yielding of our earthly existence to God's empowerment and the commitment of our life-blood to the pattern established by Christ's devotion.

Abraham was the father of those walking in faith and patterned the transaction of righteousness upon the earth. Communing with the Heavenly Father is necessary for the purpose of ascertaining His strategy before the assignment and is absolutely essential in the aftermath of victory.

How often have we interceded before a battle only to ignore commune after victory has been assured? It is quite probable that post-victory commune is more rewarding than pre-battle intercession. After all, Melchizedek arrived after the battle had been won. The representatives of the enemy arrived then, too.

Melchizedek, the king of peace, depicts the progression of righteous conquest. There must be a battle and a victory in order for peace to be declared.

FIRST ISSUANCE OF RIGHTEOUSNESS

Immediately following his fellowship with Melchizedek, Abram was led aside by God into a place where his righteous stand was first declared.

> **Genesis 15:5-6** And he brought him forth abroad, and said, Look now toward heaven, and tell the stars, if thou be able to number them: and he said unto him, So shall thy seed be. 6 And he believed in the LORD; and he counted it to him for righteousness.

Righteousness will connect the heavens and the earth and will be gained by believing things that do not seem readily apparent. Impossible promises are the foundational mortar of the creed of righteousness. In the days to come, only such impossible thinking will suffice. The kings and lords that follow Jesus must have this righteous blood flowing within them in order to empower their commitment and obedience to orders.

Partnering With The Angelic

It is vital that we perceive the connection between the stars and the earth. The stars are representative of the angels that serve God. In the Book of Revelation Jesus clearly identifies the stars as being the angels of the seven churches.

> **Revelation 1:20** The mystery of the seven stars which thou sawest in my right hand, and the seven golden candlesticks. The seven stars are the angels of the seven churches: and the seven candlesticks which thou sawest are the seven churches.

In the Book of Judges, we see that the angels cooperated with God's people in defeating a murderous Syrian General named Sisera. Although a bold woman named Jael eventually achieved his demise through a daring act, it is apparent from the Biblical account that this was the culmination of a heavenly plan.

> **Judges 5:20** They fought from heaven; the stars in their courses fought against Sisera.

There are various other passages that equate the stars with angelic beings, both good and bad. For the sake of this discussion, God was declaring to Abraham that the cause of righteousness would be accomplished by the joint venture of mankind and the angels. This tandem is reiterated time and again throughout much of the apocalyptic literature of the Bible.

PREACHING THE GOSPEL OF THE KINGDOM

A brilliant feature of this reality is found in the New Testament. Truly the work of establishing the righteous purpose of God on this planet can be summed up by what the Bible calls establishing the Kingdom of God. There is a well-known passage of scripture that speaks readily of the progression of the Kingdom of God. For much of its usage, the powerful passage in Romans 14 has been used to chastise the rich. In reality, it gives us the progression of kingdom taking.

> **Romans 14:17** For the kingdom of God is not meat and drink; but righteousness, and peace, and joy in the Holy Ghost.

We should not focus our lives on the acquisition of natural provision, but our intent should be directed toward the things of God's purpose. The Kingdom of God consists of three specific things, and the progression begins with righteousness. Righteousness is the purpose of God, and that purpose is the guideline for our life as well as for all of creation.

In order to establish righteousness in the midst of an unrighteous environment, some measure of warfare is going to have to be conducted. Warfare won yields the peace of victory. This peaceful triumph yields the joy of obedience to God's plan and purpose.

Jesus came to redeem man to God in order that man might partner with God and the angels in restoring righteousness to the planet. The rebellion of Lucifer and his fallen host, along with the sin of Adam, create the quagmire of unrighteousness that we witness in the world today. God will utilize the faithful angels and redeemed man to restore His kingdom on the earth.

What did Jesus preach before the cross during the three and a half years of His earthly ministry? Certainly His teaching must not have been overly fixated upon His death at Calvary, or the disciples and everyone else who heard Him would have understood that essential ministry more clearly. Even during the passion week the disciples seemed clueless about what was really going to happen.

We see a sterling reality about Jesus' emphasis on the righteous kingdom when we look at His initial sermons. Then we witness a progression of development regarding this gospel of the Kingdom.

- **The Gospel Of The Kingdom Redeems Agents of Righteousness**

John the Baptist prepared the way for Jesus by preaching the necessity of repenting or turning from evil in order to be right with

God. Jesus began His ministry by being baptized by John in order to "fulfill all righteousness."

> **Matthew 3:15** And Jesus answering said unto him, Suffer it to be so now: for thus it becometh us to fulfil all righteousness. Then he suffered him.

It has been well established that Jesus did not need to be forgiven of sin and that there was no repentance necessary in His life. When He proclaimed to John that righteousness was being fulfilled by virtue of His submission to immersion, He simply declared a validation of the ministry of John the Baptist. Jesus would now continue in the path of righteousness as John was shortly to be removed from the scene of public ministry.

Many lessons are revealed through an observance of this vital action. Perhaps the most dynamic was the sense of selfless timing that characterized the righteous ministry of both of these men. Repentance is only the beginning of the pathway of the Lord. In modern Christendom it is generally regarded as the culmination of service to God. When Jesus fulfilled righteousness in the Jordan River, He was only beginning His earthly ministry. In the three-plus years that followed, a transaction of repentance was not repeated again. This baptism validated the fact that repentance is only the beginning for the church.

Why is it then that Christian people are baptized and continually cured in the waters of repentance? The typical believer will hear hundreds of sermons on salvation in his lifetime and precious few concerning his duties of warring for the kingdom. Jesus fulfilled righteousness in baptismal waters. The Holy Ghost then descended upon Him as a sign of Sonship and endued Him with power.

Too many Pentecostals view the Holy Ghost as a buddy and personal valet instead of their partner and empowerment of righteousness. The Spirit of God comes for the purpose of continually perfecting our walk as a son of God and also to empower us to transact kingdom business.

> **Mark 1:14-15** Now after that John was put in prison, Jesus came into Galilee, preaching the gospel of the kingdom of God, 15 And saying, The time is fulfilled, and the kingdom of God is at hand: repent ye, and believe the gospel.

From this point of beginnings, Jesus went about preaching and teaching the Kingdom of God. In essence, He was preparing the way for the cross by declaring Kingdom principles for what man could accomplish after they were redeemed to the Father.

AGENTS OF RIGHTEOUSNESS LEARN THE PRINCIPLES OF THE KINGDOM

Once people believe in God, they have a responsibility to move within the things of the kingdom. The disciples had to learn what the Lord had to say about how the Kingdom of God operates.

> **Luke 8:1** And it came to pass afterward, that he went throughout every city and village, preaching and shewing the glad tidings of the kingdom of God: and the twelve were with him.

Not everyone will understand these concepts. Even many "Christian" people will be perplexed concerning what God is doing in the world. Only those who remain willing to leave all will be able to glean the mysteries that God is declaring regarding the Kingdom.

> **Mark 4:11-12** And he said unto them, Unto you it is given to know the mystery of the kingdom of God: but unto them that are without, all these things are done in parables: 12 That seeing they may see, and not perceive; and hearing they may hear, and not understand; lest at any time they should be converted, and their sins should be forgiven them.
>
> **Matthew 13:11** He answered and said unto them, Because it is given unto you to know the mysteries of the kingdom of heaven, but to them it is not given.

The gospel of the Kingdom is still being revealed. Many within the church wrongfully assume that we know everything that is implied by this statement. God is still revealing these truths in a timely and effective manner. Mysteries such as these involve what God is doing in this earth, and what He is transacting according to His progressive timeline.

Most of the church thinks that God has done all that He is going to do, and His next appearance will be at the rapture. This is simply not true. The gospel of the kingdom is alive today, and the agents of God Almighty are applying this message within the world.

THE GOSPEL OF THE KINGDOM CONTINUES TODAY

When the cross of Christ is preached, men and women have the opportunity to accept the saving work of the Lord Jesus Christ. This is the fantastic gift of God, and no one can follow after God without accepting Jesus as Savior. As wonderful as this truth is, the sad fact is that the message of the cross is usually all that the church knows. The general believer either preaches that message or hears it over and over again in the pew with each passing Sunday.

The cross redeems us to the Heavenly Father in order that we might serve Him. Jesus is the firstborn of many brethren. "As many as receive Him" are given power to become the sons of God. His sons are entrusted with carrying their own cross of obedience to Him. Their cross will involve the sacrifice of their lives in exchange for the purpose of God. That purpose will mightily involve the Kingdom of righteousness.

- **Agents Of Righteousness Prepare This World For The End Times**

The pre-eminent passage about preparing for the end is found in the Book of Matthew. It is the gospel of the kingdom that will bring forth the culmination of the physical world as we know it today.

> **Matthew 24:14** And this gospel of the kingdom shall be preached in all the world for a witness unto all nations; and then shall the end come.

The gospel of the kingdom will be preached to the nations. Whether this is referring to people groups or literal governmental entities, this preaching is not necessarily to the individual person.

An appreciation of this will open new vistas of understanding for the church. We realize that God desires to redeem His footstool as well as the people of the footstool.

> **Isaiah 66:1** Thus saith the Lord, The heaven is my throne, and the earth is my footstool: where is the house that ye build unto me? and where is the place of my rest?

God brings us into right relationship with Him so that we can become His partner in redeeming the earth. Mankind was created to fellowship with God and to exercise dominion within His earthly footstool. As we glean this truth, we acquire a powerful piece to the puzzle of God's revealed purpose. Righteousness is God's purpose, and the redemption of the earth was being preached by our Lord before the cross. This same message is increasingly being proclaimed by the saints today.

- **Agents Of Righteousness Partner With Angels In The Gospel Of The Kingdom**

    Angels, both good and evil, are busily warring in the battle for righteousness. In Revelation 14 a mighty angel of God is seen carrying a curious item.

    > **Revelation 14: 6** And I saw another angel fly in the midst of heaven, having the everlasting gospel to preach unto them that dwell on the earth, and to every nation, and kindred, and tongue, and people.

    This angelic sight shows us that the gospel is for people and nations. We preach this gospel to people and places on the earth. Dark angels will attempt to confuse the message of righteousness in order that their false kingdom remains undisturbed. The Word of God declares that there are doctrines of devils. Undoubtedly there is a false gospel of the kingdom which is declared by evil men in conjunction with demons.

> **Galations 1:8-9** But though we, or an angel from heaven, preach any other gospel unto you than that which we have preached unto you, let him be accursed. 9 As we said before, so say I now again, If any man preach any other gospel unto you than that ye have received, let him be accursed.

THE WAR FOR RIGHTEOUSNESS

When Abram believed God concerning the promise that involved the stars and the earth, a representative of Adam's seed first established righteousness. The patriarchs who followed in Abram's lineage established land by building altars of worship and enjoyed partnering with angels. God showed us in no uncertain terms that He is keenly interested in establishing the Kingdom of Heaven upon the earth, and He will use us to do it. Remember that when Jesus taught His disciples to pray, He began by establishing our focus on the Heavenly Father. He continued the pattern of prayer by directing our gaze to heaven so that it might be confirmed upon the earth.

Melchizedek is an essential component within the framework of our understanding of righteousness. God desires that

His children reign with Him wherever we have been assigned, and we are to conduct the Father's business through transacting righteous purpose. Melchizedek was God's representative on earth in the place of God's choosing.

God chose that Jesus should follow the Order of Melchizedek instead of that of Aaron. This is a significant fact that empowers the responsibilities of the saints. Jesus came to provide right standing before the Father through the cleansing of sin. Our Lord also came to proclaim the redemption of the planet as well as of the people.

Jesus came to provide the way to God and the possibility of sonship. His sacrifice made possible our walk of righteousness. During Jesus' earthly ministry, it was not His intention to dominate the planet. It is God's plan that we accomplish that goal, and this is part of the greater works that the saint will do in obedience to God. The saints are being directed to pathways of conquest, and in that process the enemy will be evicted from power and dominion.

King David wrote prophetically concerning Melchizedek in conjunction with the ministry of our Lord Jesus.

Psalm 110:1-7 The LORD said unto my Lord, Sit thou at my right hand, until I make thine enemies thy footstool. 2 The LORD shall send the rod of thy strength out of Zion: rule thou in the midst of

> thine enemies. 3 Thy people shall be willing in the day of thy power, in the beauties of holiness from the womb of the morning: thou hast the dew of thy youth. 4 The LORD hath sworn, and will not repent, Thou art a priest for ever after the order of Melchizedek. 5 The Lord at thy right hand shall strike through kings in the day of his wrath. 6He shall judge among the heathen, he shall fill the places with the dead bodies; he shall wound the heads over many countries. 7 He shall drink of the brook in the way: therefore shall he lift up the head.

King David was a lover of God and a warrior. Jesus is the Son of David, and He is establishing the Tabernacle of David in this hour. A tabernacle moves and so will the progression of God's righteous ways on this planet. According to Verse 2, the leading of God will often place His people in the midst of the enemy. David said in Psalm 23 that our table is prepared in the presence of our enemies. The Order of Melchizedek is a warring and communing order of priests before the Heavenly Father.

chapter 4

Recently the American Medical Association conducted research regarding the effectiveness of a popular cholesterol-reducing drug. The study concluded that the drug was highly effective toward lowering cholesterol levels. The only caveat being that for people to receive the defined results, the drug would have to actually be taken.

While we might scoff at such an obvious judgment, it is apparent that sometimes people do not do what is in their best interest. It is the same way with the church and the things of God. The Apostle Paul speaks very plainly that the grace gifts of 1 Corinthians 12 are *pneumatikos* gifts. One of the reasons that we have not seen the fullness of the gifts of the Spirit in our midst is that we have no *pnuematikos* base from which they can flow.

> **1 Corinthians 12:1** Now concerning spiritual gifts, brethren, I would not have you ignorant.

In these last days, God is opening up the themes and concepts of His Word so that His purposes might be actualized. An understanding of *pneumatikos* is bursting forth from the shadows of God's hand. We must grasp His declaration. We cannot choose to remain ignorant regarding the operation of the *pneumatikos*.

In these days, the Holy Spirit is revealing more that the Lord has in store for the church. We cannot afford a non-caring or an "if it happens, it happens" mentality. Ignorance in this instance is not bliss but folly and destruction. Hosea 4:6 states the horrible consequence of rejecting the knowledge of God:

> **Hosea 4:6** My people are destroyed for lack of knowledge: because thou hast rejected knowledge, I will also reject thee, that thou shalt be no priest to me: seeing thou hast forgotten the law of thy God, I will also forget thy children.

THE PRAYER OF THE APOSTLE PAUL

The knowledge of God is essential to our survival and growth. I do not speak of knowing about God but of knowing Him. When we know Him, we know His ways. As we learn His ways, we create the environment in which He will display His magnificence among us.

The Apostle Paul knew that the key to successfully living for God was found in living in God. As we enjoy this lifestyle and accrue His wisdom into our daily walk, we also discover the way that He would conduct His business. Paul declared that he never ceased to pray that the Colossians would come to this knowledge and that they would become proficient at the ***pneumatikos***. Think of all of the things that Paul might have prayed for in the life of this church. The most prominent need that they encountered was what

Paul daily brought before God's throne of grace. They needed the *pneumatikos*, and so do we.

> **Colossians 1:9-10** For this cause we also, since the day we heard it, do not cease to pray for you, and to desire that ye might be filled with the knowledge of his will in all wisdom and spiritual understanding; 10 That ye might walk worthy of the Lord unto all pleasing, being fruitful in every good work, and increasing in the knowledge of God;

Once you are filled with the knowledge of His will in wisdom and understanding, the result is walking worthy of the Lord, being fruitful and then increasing in His knowledge.

How Do We Learn The Spiritual Things?

> **1 Corinthians 2:13** Which things also we speak, not in the words which man's wisdom teacheth, but which the Holy Ghost teacheth; comparing spiritual things with spiritual.14 But the natural man receiveth not the things of the Spirit of God: for they are foolishness unto him: neither can he know them, because they are spiritually discerned. 15 But he that is spiritual judgeth all things, yet he himself is judged of no man. 16 For who hath known the mind of the Lord, that he may instruct him? But we have the mind of Christ.

The beauty of *pneumatikos* is that it has nothing to do with the rationale of man. In 1 Corinthians 2 Paul says that *pneumatikos* cannot be compared with human wisdom or teaching. It also cannot be judged by the comparisons of men and women to that which they have already experienced.

The *pneumatikos* is supposed to be that which dictates the rule of order within the church. Church government is currently devised and operated by the rule of man's accumulated knowledge, wisdom, and the precedent set by the cumulative experiences of the eldership. Upon observation of the scripture just quoted, these are the very things of which *pneumatikos* is comprised.

In order for the *pneumatikos* to exist as God desires, much of the religious structure will have to be modified or removed. Perhaps that is one of the reasons that Jesus continually told potential followers that they must leave everything to follow Him. For example, Matthew left the lucrative process of collecting taxes in order to follow Christ. In order to return to the principles of *pneumatikos* structure, much wealth, prestige and political influence is going to have to be jettisoned from the church. Whether this can be done or not is the significant issue before God.

How Do We Begin?

> **1 Corinthians 15:44-46** It is sown a natural body; it is raised a spiritual body. There is a

> natural body, and there is a spiritual body. 45 And so it is written, The first man Adam was made a living soul; the last Adam was made a quickening spirit. 46 Howbeit that was not first which is spiritual, but that which is natural; and afterward that which is spiritual.

The **spiritual** springs forth from the natural! Thank God for the assurance found within this verse! It gives hope to all of us, especially since the majority of us are in the natural most of the time. What a perfect climate to begin believing God for the ***pneumatikos***. The quickening influence of our Lord Jesus will help us to welcome the ***pneumatikos*** into our lives and churches. We must start by interceding before the Father in order to obtain the fullness of His purpose and promise.

PAUL'S CONCLUSION

The apostle recognizes that not all people are going to desire the ***pneumatikos***. There will be some who simply do not care to seek God for such an establishment. ***Pneumatikos*** speaks of an ever-changing environment that is dictated by God, and this can be very unsettling to those who desire to be in control. In 1 Corinthians 14 Paul writes that those that would be ignorant will ignore God's current ways and will choose to refrain from participating in His present move.

> **1 Corinthians 14: 37-38** If any man think himself to be a prophet, or spiritual, let him acknowledge that the things that I write unto you are the commandments of the Lord. 38 But if any man be ignorant, let him be ignorant.

"Let him be ignorant" literally means that he should be allowed to remain a receptacle of an unchanging environment, like a vase. When we consider what a vase does, we recognize that it is a fixed structure that holds placid liquid, preserving the bud of yesterday's flower. God desires for us to be trees of righteousness, living branches full of fruit! Not a display of dying flowers from the most recent harvest.

Thankfully, those who move with the Lord will be alive to what God is saying today. There will be a wondrous stirring within them concerning the things that God is doing and revealing. The ***pneumatikos*** is a prophetic unit that welcomes the new and fresh things that God is illuminating.

THE COST

> **Romans 15:27** It hath pleased them verily; and their debtors they are. For if the Gentiles have been made partakers of their spiritual things, their duty is also to minister unto them in carnal things.

1 Corinthians 9:11 If we have sown unto you spiritual things, is it a great thing if we shall reap your carnal things.

Paul wrote to the Romans and Corinthians about their responsibilities within the Body of Christ. During that day, there was great financial risk to becoming a Christian. For the Jew, a decision to follow Christ could mean complete rejection from the social and economic framework of society. Additionally, there was governmental, spiritual and climatic oppression against the people of God in several cities.

These two passages say that whenever a person becomes a partaker in the things of *pneumatikos*, part of that responsibility will be financial in scope. This involves philanthropic ministry, but it also speaks of the overall concept of committing everything that we are and have to God.

As the love of money is the root of all evil, so the yielding of money to God will provide a strong footing for the removal of evil. Gaining freedom in this area will release tremendous power within your life and ministry.

Reflection

How do you answer the prevailing question of this chapter? Are you willing to give whatever it takes in order to fulfill the call to *pneumatikos*? In order to gain this place in God, it will cost you many things that you might hold dear at this hour. Financial clout, political posture, societal influence, opinions and approval of others: all of these things, and more, are going to be required of you.

> **Mark 10:29-30** And Jesus answered and said, Verily I say unto you, There is no man that hath left house, or brethren, or sisters, or father, or mother, or wife, or children, or lands, for my sake, and the gospel's, 30 But he shall receive an hundredfold now in this time, houses, and brethren, and sisters, and mothers, and children, and lands, with persecutions; and in the world to come eternal life.

chapter 5

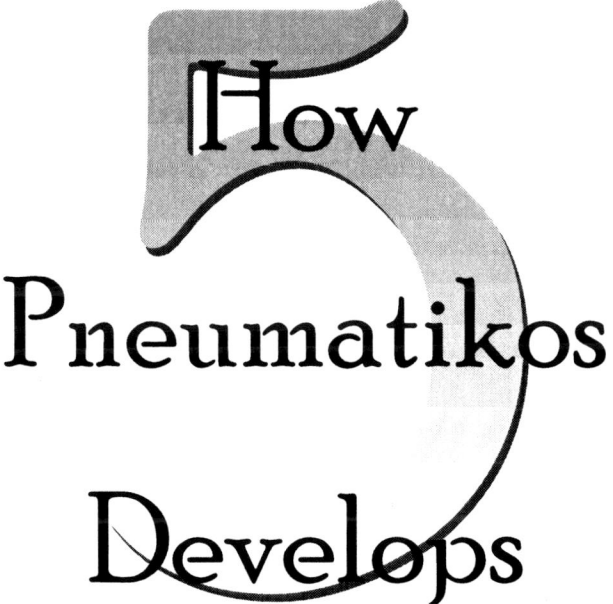

How Pneumatikos Develops

Beginning to walk in the things of the Lord is simply that, a beginning. We have a responsibility to grow and develop. The growth process of *pneumatikos* is plainly outlined within the Bible.

As soon as we are born into this world, we are allowed to receive the nourishment of milk. Every parent looks for the day that their child will progress into solid foods because this denotes healthy growth. Sadly, this normal desire is not readily followed within the church.

Within the general structure, there are many abandoned children. These well-meaning people walk up an aisle, make a commitment to God and think that they are included in all things spiritual. From that point, whether they progress into maturity, or not, is inconsequential to them and many of their leaders. Tragic!

Paul wrote to the Corinthians that he longed to be able to speak with them as adults in the Lord. This church had entered into some of the more complex things of the Spirit. Their challenge was that they would not submit to what it took to be included within the ranks of the *pneumatikos*. Paul specifically addresses this problem and continues to instruct them concerning this failure.

PROGRESSIONS OF NOURISHMENT – MILK UNTO MEAT

> **1 Corinthians 3:1-2** And I, brethren, could not speak unto you as unto spiritual, but as unto carnal, even as unto babes in Christ. 2 I have fed you with milk, and not with meat: for hitherto ye were not able to bear it, neither yet now are ye able.

Paul speaks of three different groups: those that are carnal, those that are babes in Christ, and those that are *pneumatikos*. Those that are carnal represent believers that are oriented to the flesh. Those that are babes in Christ represent those who had not progressed into the deeper things of the Lord. Paul wanted to talk to them as *pneumatikos*; and even though he started them on this process, they did not continue.

NOURISHMENT – MEAT, DRINK, AND ROCK

> **1 Corinthians 10:1-4** Moreover, brethren, I would not that ye should be ignorant, how that all our fathers were under the cloud, and all passed through the sea; 2 And were all baptized unto Moses in the cloud and in the sea; 3 And did all eat the same spiritual meat; 4 And did all drink the same spiritual drink: for they drank of that spiritual Rock that followed them: and that Rock was Christ.

When the children of Israel were delivered out of Egypt and began their wilderness wandering, they all ate the same ***pneumatikos*** meat and drank the same ***pneumatikos*** drink of that ***pneumatikos*** rock that followed them, and that rock was Christ. They began walking as spirit people following the cloud of the glory of the Lord. God wanted them to progress even further as a nation of mighty people in Him.

Note carefully the progression:

- The people recognized that they were slaves to the world and to themselves.
- God wanted to move them into freedom as well as nationhood.
- Moses was called as a voice of deliverance, and the people believed the revelation of the Word of the Lord.
- When they believed, God demonstrated the miraculous. The people were "baptized" in the miraculous atmosphere of His presence and power.
- They were all in unity: eating meat of provision that gave strength, insight, and direction. These people drank of a deep relationship with Christ, which is the embodiment of the Holy Ghost within a person that is called and submitted to God.

God wants us to walk as spirit people today. We begin by hearing the Word and believing. No matter where you are, God can deliver you from carnal focus and begin the process of transforming you into someone that He can use.

NOURISHMENT – THE NECESSITY OF THE LAW

You can remove people from bondage, but you must also remove the bondage from the people. Bondage represents old mindsets. The children of Israel that followed Moses through the wilderness were free from slavery but were never really free from the bondages within themselves. As a result, they were regularly disrespectful to Moses, and they murmured continually against him and the Lord. Also, they pined for their former life and forsook the Lord to worship the gods of the land. In short, they missed it entirely.

Romans 7:14 For we know that the law is spiritual: but I am carnal, sold under sin.

Since the people themselves were yet sold to their own sins, they continually missed the mark to which God was calling. This passage says that the law was *pneumatikos*. The **law**, or *nomos*, meant that the people had to be fed continually as animals that receive parceled nourishment. It literally means that God could only distribute His Spirit in very controlled and measured allotments. A regulated procedure of heavenly or *pneumatikos* things was all that they could tolerate. This suspended blessing was not able to change their hearts, and they died without stepping into the promise.

When the children of Israel left Egypt, they were a fearful bunch that could not conceive of God granting them victory in the promised land. This thought was born out in the comments of the spies that reported to Moses. For forty years God tried to teach them His ways. Due to the fact that they remained unregenerate in their minds, they gave place to murmuring, and God gave them over to the destroyer.

> **1 Corinthians 10:10** Neither murmur ye, as some of them also murmured, and were destroyed of the destroyer.

THE PROGRESSION AS OUTLINED TO ST. PETER

In the last chapter of the Gospel of Saint John, Peter is asked a series of questions by the Lord Jesus. Within this interchange, Peter was being queried as to his own devotion to the Lord but was also being shown the way that sheep grow and feed.

> **John 21:15-18** So when they had dined, Jesus saith to Simon Peter, Simon, son of Jonas, lovest thou me more than these? He saith unto him, Yea, Lord; thou knowest that I love thee. He saith unto him, Feed my lambs. 16 He saith to him again the

> second time, Simon, son of Jonas, lovest thou me? He saith unto him, Yea, Lord; thou knowest that I love thee. He saith unto him, Feed my sheep. 17 He saith unto him the third time, Simon, son of Jonas, lovest thou me? Peter was grieved because he said unto him the third time, Lovest thou me? And he said unto him, Lord, thou knowest all things; thou knowest that I love thee. Jesus saith unto him, Feed my sheep. 18 Verily, verily, I say unto thee, When thou wast young, thou girdedst thyself, and walkedst whither thou wouldest: but when thou shalt be old, thou shalt stretch forth thy hands, and another shall gird thee, and carry thee whither thou wouldest not.

A powerful truth is hidden within these verses, and it has to do with the development of the deep things of the Lord. In the English translation, it would appear that Jesus is repeatedly asking Peter the same thing. A careful study of the original Greek will testify to a marvelous pursuit by our Lord's questioning methods.

The first two times that Jesus inquires as to whether Peter loves Him, He asks about the measure of *agape* within Peter. In effect, He wanted to know if Peter was motivated by the purpose of the Father to provide hand-feeding for babies until they grew into mature animals that could feed in the pastures to which they were led.

To both questions, Peter answers by saying that he is a friend, or *phileo*, of Jesus. A friend in scripture is a person that can be entrusted with the heartfelt needs of another. To be a friend of Jesus would be tantamount to partnering in the maturation of people and purpose.

For the self-sufficient Peter, this process had been hard to accept. Through the years with Jesus, Peter had become submitted to obeying God in this pursuit rather than simply taking care of himself. Now comes the third question, and it involves a facet of Peter's existence that had not yet been addressed.

This third question does not ask Peter if he was filled with *agape*, as the first two questions had inquired. Instead, Jesus asked Peter if he was really willing to be a true friend, or *phileo*, to Him. This anointed question grieved Peter as it prophetically touched the core of his identity.

The reason for this deep searching within the heart of Peter was that Jesus says that to be the utmost friend of God, Peter would now need to bring maturing sheep into a place where they could be taught the power principles of the Kingdom of God. In truth, Peter was now being asked to open himself and share the deeper things of his life to maturing individuals.

It was one thing when this provision of fodder was being given to babies. It is quite another to provide fodder for people that are used to fending for themselves. Not only does Peter have to give with more humility and service, but he now has to provide insights that had been treasures in his own life.

Peter was being told by the Lord that to be the friend of God, upon which the church would be built, he would have to tend to babies, lead them to maturity, and then humbly open himself to the mature that they might become like him. Jesus said in another passage that a good shepherd will give all that he has for the sheep. To develop *pneumatikos*, the *pneumatikos* will have to give of themselves in total measure.

> **John 10:11** I am the good shepherd: the good shepherd giveth his life for the sheep.

The feeding process outlined goes like this:

1. Fodder means to provide ready food for lambs.
2. Pasture means to lead more mature sheep to a place of safety and grazing.
3. Fodder means to lead more mature sheep to a place where specified nourishment could be provided.

This is simply how people should grow. They begin as babies that are in need of constant provision and supervision. They then learn to follow and utilize the surroundings wherein they have been led. At this point mature people are fed nutrition for the purposes of them growing into a higher dimension of existence.

Imparting to the mature believer is an essential step of ***pneumatikos.***

IMPARTATION

The last phase of the progression that Jesus outlined before Peter is defined in this passage from Romans 1.

> **Romans 1:11** For I long to see you, that I may impart unto you some spiritual gift, to the end ye may be established.

A continuing dilemma for Paul was one that involved what he was able to release into the lives of people. Many times within the Word of the Lord, Paul would lament the fact that he really wanted to give something of **spiritual** merit to people but was unable to do so because of their immaturity or lack of development.

For the progression that Jesus taught Peter, there is a steady development of babies from adolescence to maturity and reproduction. Sadly these levels are not inevitable within the lives of believers. Some people remain entrenched within the realm of childish things while others progress rapidly within the things of God.

There is an unparalleled excitement in communicating the deep things of God. The third level of Peter's progression is mirrored here in Paul's desire to impart **spiritual**, or *pneumatikos*, gifts. This transference of the *pneumatikos* will happen in differing ways. Sometimes it will be to an entire grouping of spiritual ones as is the case in this passage. Other times, it will be on an individual basis. A case in point was when Paul ministered to Timothy, his son in the faith.

Pneumatikos giftings will also be utilized to augment the process of what God is already doing within the heart of a saint. Often there is the transference of a burst of power that is needed for a particular hurdle. At times an element of spiritual input will serve as a needed catalyst to effect a transaction on their behalf.

In this instance in the Book of Romans, Paul says that the *pneumatikos* gift will serve to establish the church. Establishing involves a measure of productivity and reproduction that can only occur at a mature level of development. If people are not developing into higher levels of spiritual maturity, *pneumatikos* establishment cannot transpire. If there is no *pneumatikos* in place, the greater realms of establishment of the things of God cannot materialize. Either scenario will hinder the work of the Lord.

Established believers and churches will grow in the things of the Spirit. As this develops, there is a necessity for *pneumatikos* supervision and training. The two elements go hand in hand and are essential to the life of the mature church. Nonetheless, these giftings cannot be granted to those who are not ready to receive them.

chapter 6

Pneumatikos Ministry Within the Church

1 Corinthians 12:1 Now concerning spiritual gifts, brethren, I would not have you ignorant.

At the very outset of Paul's treatise regarding spiritual gifts in 1 Corinthians, he tells the church to be careful not to limit their understanding of the things of the Spirit of God. Ignorance in this passage does not mean a lack of learning. It has been said that there is no difference between a person that can't read a book and the person that won't read a book. In decrying ignorance, Paul is speaking to the capacity of selective ignorance, those who refuse to enter the atmosphere and process of becoming aware.

Additionally, the word for spiritual gifts in this verse is *pneumatikos* and is not the same as *charis*, or grace. In most circles of interpretation, a confusing of these two Greek terms within the context of their usage has resulted in miscommunication of God's true message.

A grace gift is different from a *pnuematikos* gift. Grace gifts are generally personal in nature whether for the individual person or the specific place or moment. *Pneumatikos* gifts have to do with the overall positioning of a people in God and will align very closely with God's purpose. Another way to say it is that grace gifts will usually address specific moments and stages, while *pnuematikos* gifts are wisdom oriented.

Paul writes that we should not lose sight of what God is doing, and why. The overall picture should be viewed whenever we consider anything that God asks of us. We are responsible to be proper stewards of the mysteries that He has revealed to us, as well as the purpose for which those things have been shown.

An undue focus upon grace gifts can lead us to a very selfish mode of existence. It can also yield a shortsightedness that can prove costly in the overall depiction and pursuit of God's purpose in our church and life. Grace gifts gratify the moment and provide promotion into new terrain and environment, while *pneumatikos* gifts help to wisely establish us in that terrain.

PNEUMATIKOS AS JUDGE

> **1 Corinthians 2:15** But he that is spiritual judgeth all things, yet he himself is judged of no man. But the natural man receiveth not the things of the Spirit of God: for they are foolishness unto him: neither can he know them, because they are spiritually discerned. 16 For who hath known the mind of the Lord, that he may instruct him? But we have the mind of Christ.

This passage graphically displays the way that the *pneumatikos* priesthood flows before the Father on behalf of the church. The mind of Christ is the mental perception of what God wants to accomplish through the Holy Ghost in the world today. This involves the counsel of the Father and is not open to the scrutiny of man's consent.

Within the next several pages of this book, we will discover the absolute importance of the role of the ***pneumatikos*** in gleaning what is and is not prudent within the operation of the church. Sometimes the opposition to the flow of the Spirit will come from outside the camp. At other times, the ***pneumatikos*** will be required to restrain gifted individuals who have lost track of timing or are placing an undue emphasis upon an emotional insistence for grace gifts.

Humility to the authority structure that God has placed within the house is essential to the welcoming of the deep things of God. Submission to authority is essential in all aspects of the spirit realm. In the past, the enemy has successfully pressed this issue, and in the process has restrained the move of God's Spirit. In essence, it is all a matter of preferring one another and walking in humility. Without humility, there will be no free flow of grace. Rest assured that God will honor His authority structure, and the ***pneumatikos*** are a vital supervisory element within that structure.

JURISDICTION

> **1 Corinthians 2:13** Which things also we speak, not in the words which man's wisdom teacheth, but which the Holy Ghost teacheth; comparing spiritual things with spiritual.

It is imperative that we compare *pneumatikos* things with *pneumatikos*. *Sugkrino,* or **comparing**, is that process wherein we take one item or aspect and combine it with another. Wisdom consists of knowing what goes where, but this ability involves more than just wisdom. *Pneumatikos* is an administrator of the things of the Lord.

The *pneumatikos* comparison will not be subject to man's wisdom or teaching. Taking this in its proper context, the fresh wind of the Spirit cannot be evaluated by the way things have always been or according to the most recent doctrinal statement. *Pneumatikos* has a way of agreeing with the doctrines that have gone before without being subject to the old ways that formed them. This is how we can forget the things that are behind and press on toward the higher. It is also how we can align with Hebrews 6 as we leave doctrinal things to press on unto perfection.

This is a very serious business that will be scrutinized by the establishment while at the same time being attacked by the enemy.

Pneumatikos is that exquisite blend of foundation and fresh structure, security and faith's risk, old and new. In order to do this properly, a miracle must occur. People have to grow strong in the Lord while at the same time humbling themselves before recognized leadership.

How many times has the church suffered because there has been no such office within the house of the Lord? Traditionally, when someone has received an insight from God, the enemy will attempt to engender pride or presumption in the natural mind. The timing of the Lord is often missed. Additionally, there is no opportunity for "comparing" ***pneumatikos*** with ***pneumatikos*** because individuals have rarely been willing to submit their revelation to anyone or anything. We have not learned what it means to "know in part and prophesy in part." ***Pneumatikos*** brings these parts into focus by comparing **spiritual** things with **spiritual**.

Agreement of insight is essential to progress, but it is rare to find this operating in a successful manner. If pride does not destroy the process, a lack of confidence in God's ability to speak through us will doom the progression.

When my church began to seek the Lord in fresh ways, God told me something that has profoundly influenced our local body and me. It had to do with knowing our purpose as well as assimilating insights from other places where God was moving in distinct ways. The Lord told me that if I would trust His individual purpose for us and respect His revealed purpose to others, everything would be all right. In the church we generally fall into one side or the other. We are either blown about by every wind or not affected by the wind at all. The reasons for this are myriad and stem from ignorance, jealousy, competition, emulation or any number of other variant insecurities.

So what do we do with a passage such as the one found in 1 Corinthians 2?

1 Corinthians 2:15 But he that is spiritual judgeth all things, yet he himself is judged of no man.

What about a parallel passage found in 1 John?

1 John 2:27 But the anointing which ye have received of him abideth in you, and ye need not that any man teach you: but as the same anointing teacheth you of all things, and is truth, and is no lie, and even as it hath taught you, ye shall abide in him.

When Paul says that the *pneumatikos* individual will "judge" all things, he utilizes the Greek word *anakrino*. This is an investigative word that speaks of obtaining information from many sources in order to glean the full picture. In this respect, the information that is gleaned will come from the Holy Spirit; and as we wait upon Him, our understanding will be comprehensive in scope. When it says the *pneumatikos* is not to be judged by any man, it is truly a testament that what God is doing through the *pneumatikos* may not have been seen or known before. This may therefore not be a part of the spectrum of the knowledge of man.

The *anakrino* will provide much information for the comparing, or *sugkrino,* anointing to prosper. The key factor is that these points of instruction are discovered and facilitated by the *pneumatikos*.

Paul wrote to the Corinthians that the *pneumatikos* should receive direction from the Lord within a framework of accountability. By saying that this group is judged of no man, he was literally saying that revelation from God does not rely upon the approval of man for validity. John proceeds to say that the Holy Spirit will reveal God's heart as you abide in Him. 1 John 2:26 is the pretext of this and instructs that you should be wary of those that would attempt to proffer a parallel, but wrong, pathway.

So Paul and John tell us that we need to seek the Lord in both an intimately personal and corporate setting. This is where the *sugkrino* anointing assumes its prominent place. We are much in need of knowing our place in the Lord and trusting therein while also aligning with influences of His choosing.

THUS SAITH THE LORD!

How many times has that phrase been spoken within Pentecostal circles and corporate gatherings? Have we really witnessed a true rendition of the meaning within our churches? Look closely at the following passage and view it in context as well as in light of our current discussion.

> **1 Corinthians 14:29-33** Let the prophets speak two or three, and let the other judge. 30 If any thing be revealed to another that sitteth by, let the first hold his peace. 31 For ye may all prophesy one by one, that all may learn, and all may be comforted. 32 And the spirits of the prophets are subject to the prophets. 33 For God is not the author of confusion, but of peace, as in all churches of the saints.

Verse 29 says that the other, or different, should judge our prophetic word. This means that when a word comes forth, it should be submitted to a differing source within that same ***pneumatikos*** for a proper examination and evaluation. 1 Thessalonians 5 says that we should not despise prophecy but should hold fast to that which is good. Within the process of judging a word, we need to recognize that there may be a measure of human alloy mixed in with the declaration. We must look carefully and redeem the pure and good from each expression. The ***sugkrino*** will not only amalgam various words but will review each word for clarity and true meaning.

Generally we have quoted Verse 32 in the singular, telling a prophet that he or she can restrain their "word" for proper timing of utterance. While true, there is also a more prominent meaning to this verse. The designation for prophet is not singular but plural.

Literally, the wind of God that is moving among His people will be subject to whatever the people will allow Him to do in them. If there is a humility and sensitivity in judging how that wind is blowing, there is no limit to what can occur at a gathering of God's people. If there is a desire to follow hard after God without giving way to the weariness of the flesh, we can pursue from a thirty-fold return to a sixty-fold return. If we continue to allow Judah praise to plow and do not become overly concerned with prematurely enjoying the fruits of what has already been given, we can move fully into the hundred-fold intent of the Lord for our time in Him.

CORRECTION AND RESTORATION

> **Galatians 6:1** Brethren, if a man be overtaken in a fault, ye which are spiritual, restore such an one

in the spirit of meekness; considering thyself, lest thou also be tempted.

We would be remiss if we did not focus on the most prominent reason for *pneumatikos* failure. This concept is clearly defined in the Greek word translated as **overtaken**. **Overtaken**, or *prolambano*, means to take, eat or arrive too soon or out of sync with the proper order. This is chiefly an issue of improper timing.

Timing is essential to everything in life, but especially in the life of the Spirit. Waiting upon the Father for direction in timing is essential to the life of every believer. It would seem then that timing is of the essence for the *pneumatikos*. God places situations and people within our lives for the purpose of enforcing that education.

Those who wanted to move ahead of the proper cadence of obedience continually beset King David. In resisting the temptations found within warriors like Abishai, the king perfected patience before God. Patient adherence to the heartbeat of the Father caused David to gain great favor with Him. Impatience caused other kings in the Old Testament to lose their throne and life. Saul could not wait for the arrival of the prophet Samuel and was stripped of his crown. Josiah did not wait for the Lord to deliver Egypt into his hand and subsequently surrendered his very life due to impetuousness.

During the temptation in the wilderness, the enemy pressed the issue of moving ahead of God's perfect timetable. At the wedding of Cana, the site of His first miracle, Jesus spoke of His need to be in exact harmony with the timing of His Father in Heaven.

> **John 2:4-5** Jesus saith unto her, Woman, what have I to do with thee? mine hour is not yet come.
> 5 His mother saith unto the servants, Whatsoever he saith unto you, do it.

Throughout His ministry the people surrounding Jesus continually pressed this issue. In fact, after the resurrection the Lord commanded the disciples to go to Jerusalem and *wait* for the promise of the Father. That promise did not arrive until the Day of Pentecost was fully come. When questioned about the time of the end, Jesus referred the question to the wisdom of the Father.

The Apostle Paul identified the first sign of an apostolic ministry to be that of waiting upon the Lord in patience. This trait superceded and made possible the signs, wonders and mighty deeds.

> **2 Corinthians 12:12** Truly the signs of an apostle were wrought among you in all patience, in signs, and wonders, and mighty deeds.

If the enemy cannot stop a mighty man or woman from moving forward, he will attempt to influence them to veer off target. Failing in these, his last resort is to encourage failure in timing. Think of it. The enemy cannot keep the *pneumatikos* from moving forward. If they are gleaning the mind of Christ, he cannot keep them from knowing the objective. Satan will attempt to influence presumption and pretentious influences to corrupt the person and plan of God. You can have the right thing at the wrong time and be just as wrong as if you had the wrong thing.

How crafty our adversary! The *pneumatikos* must be bold and avant-garde. However, this daring must be established within the mantle of essential timing and obedience. This priesthood must remain sensitive to the heart of God and to His overall purpose. The *pneumatikos* plays a vital role in gathering together to form a protective, restorative influence whenever someone varies from the proper assimilation and application of the mind of Christ.

Write this down and do not ever forget it: Wherever the Lord moves, there will be challenge and opposition. Much of the challenge will come from the inherent failure of human beings to handle the weight of responsibility. When people make mistakes, and they will, the *pneumatikos* are essential for rectification and restoration. As people press through within the heavenlies, the enemy perceives their entry into areas where he has only seen a few go, and even into some realms where he has never seen a human being. The enemy will oppose this progression with due force.

Reflecting once again on the teaching of Galatians 6, the ***pneumatikos*** who are close to God's heartbeat need to surround the errant one like a cast over a broken arm and restore them in meekness. This must be done with humility, grace, and seasoning to avoid a similar downfall in their own life. An important characteristic of a ***pneumatikos*** individual is humility. This individual will not proceed with a wide swathe in the name of correction. After all, this passage is speaking of brothers, even fellow ***pneumatikos***, who have been overtaken and missed the mark.

PRESBYTERY

> **1 Corinthians 14:37** If any man think himself to be a prophet, or spiritual, let him acknowledge that the things that I write unto you are the commandments of the Lord.

Just prior to this verse, Paul was teaching about how valuable the prophetic voice is in the church, and that we should strive to prophesy. He says that we must have prophecy in the church because it stirs up, lifts up and builds up. Paul was also teaching about the office of prophecy and says that if anyone thinks himself to be a prophet, or ***pneumatikos***, then he will testify to the truth of the teaching.

There is a clearly defined address to the prophet and to a different group known to Paul as ***pneumatikos.*** These two groups are not the same, but they will operate in tandem with each other.

Many of you may have interpreted this passage to mean that Paul was talking to those who "just think they are so spiritual," or who display a haughty, "holier than thou" attitude. Since we did not include ourselves in that category, we would just skip over the passage and move on without attempting to interpret it. Paul is not maligning the prophet or the ***pneumatikos*** individual but is appealing to them. He says, "This is the way the church should be run, and if there is anybody in the church who knows themselves to be a prophet or to function in this realm of the ***pneumatikos***, then let him acknowledge the things that I write unto you as being the commandments of the Lord. If anybody elects to dwell in ignorance, just let them be that way."

Wisdom

Colossians 1:9 For this cause we also, since the day we heard it, do not cease to pray for you, and

> to desire that ye might be filled with the knowledge of his will in all wisdom and spiritual understanding.

There was a passionate longing on behalf of the apostle for the Colossians to acquire wisdom and **spiritual** understanding. The Apostle Paul was so driven by this desire that he offered up ceaseless prayer concerning this necessity. Are we equally desirous of receiving this within our churches? Do we intercede continually for this attribute?

Pneumatikos understanding addresses the grasping of what is available from the Lord for the church. It also details an existing understanding of the circumstances of the spirit realm and how the church is interacting therein. It further clarifies who we are in the Lord, and what our place is within His Body.

Wisdom is that facet which speaks of timing and influence. The proper understanding can be wasted because of untimely expression or implementation. Often the Father will grant understanding simply for our edification and training and not necessarily for immediate application on our part. Wisdom will help us to glean His purpose and timing. Operating in this understanding yields a climate of prosperity and blessing.

Pneumatikos individuals had a very real function within the New Testament church. They understood progressive moves of the

Spirit and had deep understanding of spiritual matters. There is a close harmony that exists between prophetic words within ongoing church life, the office of the prophet and the *pneumatikos*. Let us not dwell in ignorance regarding this vital understanding.

chapter 7

Worshipful Warriors

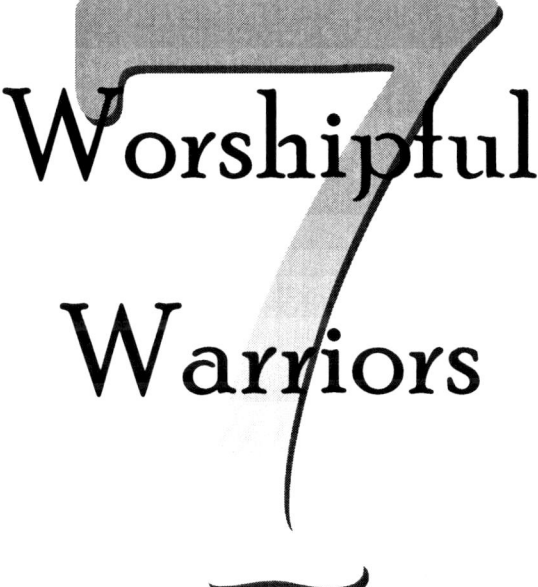

When we view the ministry of the ***pneumatikos*** and saints throughout the Book of Revelation, we see some wondrous things in conjunction with what we learned about the Order of Melchizedek in Chapter 3. Particularly, the saint will be a person that wars by virtue of his commune with the Heavenly Father. Directives from the Father will flow from that place of commune, and the saints will go forth as the tribe of Judah with harps and creative expression in their hands.

The place of this creative warfare is depicted in the tribe of Judah. Jesus was born into that lineage and became the Lion of the Tribe of Judah. Prophetically, Judah must pioneer the new planting and ways of God.

> **Hosea 10:11...**I will make Ephraim to ride; Judah shall plow, and Jacob shall break his clods.

Judah was regularly chosen by God to be placed in the front of the army in warfare. This is strategic placement in many ways, but one in particular stands above the rest.

Why did God choose to send His Son in the line of Judah instead of Joseph? After all, Joseph was the paragon of virtue among the offspring of Jacob, and Judah lacked propriety in several important ways.

For that matter, why did God choose a lineage for His Son that was populated by inconsistency and notable debauchery? Why was Jesus born in a smallish locale amidst a humble family and surroundings? The answer to these questions provide a major insight into the plan of God.

God could have chosen an absolutely perfect environment for the implementation of His plan. According to the justice of God, it would only be equitable to defeat iniquity by sending people that continually rely upon Him for the overcoming of iniquity in their lives. God is fair, even with the enemy.

At the head of God's conquering army is a group of people that readily admit that their personal righteousness is as filthy rags. They have been forgiven much, and subsequently they love God with everything that is within them. Their bright light of worship and devotion shines as a testament of total dependence upon God for everything that they need.

The enemy that stands in opposition to this army of God cannot accuse the Lord of stacking the deck against Him. God has sent an unlikely group of victors to do His bidding. Into an iniquitous world God sends a people that have known iniquity. They have overcome iniquity by the blood of the Lamb, and they can apply that overcoming power into this sinful world. God's plan is flawless!

> **Judges 20:18** And the children of Israel arose, and went up to the house of God, and asked counsel of God, and said, Which of us shall go up first to the battle against the children of Benjamin? And the LORD said, Judah shall go up first.

It would seem that the power of God is delegated to those that know the wonder and majesty of intercession and open devotion to God. When we see the kings and lords in heaven, they have harps for worship and bowls that represent collective incense of intercession and commune with God.

> **Revelation 5:8-10** And when he had taken the book, the four beasts and the four and twenty elders fell down before the Lamb, having every one of them harps, and golden vials full of odours, which are the prayers of saints. 9 And they sung a new song, saying, Thou art worthy to take the book, and to open the seals thereof: for thou wast slain, and has redeemed us to God by thy blood out of every kindred, and tongue, and people, and nation; 10 And has made us unto our God kings and priests: and we shall reign on the earth.

The four beasts are living beings that are extremely large and well-developed in dimension. The eyes that encompass their countenance represent the monitoring and overseeing eyes of God. God's eyes search the planet for those that will worship Him, and

His eyes are always on the righteous. To call these creatures "beasts" conveys an incomplete picture because they are anything but grotesque or abnormal in proportion or behavior. Ezekiel describes these marvelous creations of God as "living creatures."

> **Ezekiel 1:5-14** Also out of the midst thereof came the likeness of four living creatures. And this was their appearance; they had the likeness of a man. 6 And every one had four faces, and every one had four wings. 7 And their feet were straight feet; and the sole of their feet was like the sole of a calf's foot: and they sparkled like the colour of burnished brass. 8 And they had the hands of a man under their wings on their four sides; and they four had their faces and their wings. 9 Their wings were joined one to another; they turned not when they went; they went every one straight forward. 10 As for the likeness of their faces, they four had the face of a man, and the face of a lion, on the right side: and they four had the face of an ox on the left side; they four also had the face of an eagle. 11 Thus were their faces: and their wings were stretched upward; two wings of every one were joined one to another, and two covered their bodies. 12 And they went every one straight forward: whither the spirit was to go, they went; and they turned not when they went. 13 As for the likeness of the living creatures, their appearance was like burning coals of fire, and like the appearance of lamps: it went up and down among the living creatures; and the fire was bright, and out of the fire went forth lightning. 14 And the living creatures ran and returned as the appearance of a flash of lightning.

Anyone might tell from this vivid description that these living creatures are beautiful and wondrous to behold. Note the fluidity of motion and alacrity of speed with which he defines their graceful movements. They are similar to the seraphim in that they conduct themselves as the fire of the Lord. They also possess other qualities that are worth noting in this discussion.

They have four faces, and the positioning and selection of each of these is essential to understand their importance. Not only do they have eyes that encompass the creation of God, but on the right side of their face they depict a man and a lion. The man and lion speak of the individual that will align with the Lion of the Tribe of Judah. Being on the right represents a grasping of prophetic vision. The ox on the left speaks of the ability to apply strength and tenacity to the fulfillment of the vision. The eagle represents wisdom and overall insight in this pursuit. Also, within the eagle representation is the idea of resilience in the advent of any storm or adverse wind current. Keen insight, speed of flight and acquisition of sustenance are watchwords for the eagle. These magnificent creatures move with the Spirits of God as defined by the movement of the wind in verse 12 and the lamps in verse 13.

What place do the elders hold in conjunction with the four beasts? In verse 13, the creatures are depicted as being burning coals and that they move in conjunction with the lively stones of God or the saints. The elders coordinate these efforts of the saints.

The elders have traditionally been classified as "heavenly senators." This designation is tidy but not really functional. According to Revelation 5, they sing the song of those redeemed by the blood of the Lamb of God.

The elders consist of some well-recognized patriarchs as well as other saints that are less known by the masses. There are some elders that are walking the face of this earth today. Additionally, the elders assist in the development of the saints on earth that form the ranks of those that serve the Lord God.

A fuller depiction of these individuals will be addressed in Chapter 10. For this current chapter, it is important that we understand that all of the elders and beasts possess harps and vials. In many ways the elders are the heavenly ***pneumatikos***.

THE SIGNIFICANCE OF VIALS

As the harp speaks of creative expressions of warfare and worship, the vial speaks of intercession that is as incense before the Lord. Nobody will ever be called as a saint or ***pneumatikos*** unless they are a devoted worshipper of God.

The vial, or bowl, speaks of God's ability to coordinate intercession during the entire development of His purpose. In Acts, the angel told Cornelius that his prayers had continually risen before God as a memorial. Daniel was informed that his prayers were registered on the first day of intercession and were considered by the Lord throughout the twenty-one days of his fast. Similarly, the prayers of the saints are being offered now for the time of the end. This is vividly portrayed in the following passage.

> **Revelation 8:4-6** And the smoke of the incense, which came with the prayers of the saints, ascended up before God out of the angel's hand. 5 And the angel took the censer, and filled it with fire of the altar, and cast it into the earth: and there were voices, and thunderings, and lightnings, and an earthquake. 6 And the seven angels who had the seven trumpets prepared themselves to sound.

The plagues that follow this release of accumulated intercession are militarily precise in dismantling the controlling powers of evil that yet defile the heavens and earth. Many saints are at this moment conducting intercessory battle against the influences that are listed in Revelation 8 and 9.[2]

---

[2] This topic is found in the book entitled **Princes of the Dark Realm** by Ron Crawford, Pneumatikos Publishing.

chapter 8

Creative Worship of the Pneumatikos

As priests of the Father continually glean understanding of His heart and ways, these truths will then be prophetically expressed toward the goal of making His thoughts known within the church. Some might feel that prophecy is a mysterious and extreme function, but true prophetic ministry will make the complicated seem very plain to even the most elemental of people.

The ***pneumatikos*** should bring forth whatever is upon the heart of the Father. Sometimes that will be a present truth in ***rhema*** fashion. Other times it will be a startlingly clear revelation that depicts and explains a previously unclear or unseen truth. There are songs that are issued from the throne, and the ***pneumatikos*** will give birth to them. Whether it is song, ***rhema,*** or instruction, the ***oide pneumatikos*** will follow a pattern that is clearly demarked in the scripture.

WORSHIP THROUGH ARTISTIC EXPRESSION

Creativity will be the mark of prophetic inclination among the ***pneumatikos***. Foundation will be necessary, but it serves as a solid base for the purpose of pressing forth into creative revelation and expression of God's ways.

One of the ways God desires to declare Himself is through the song of His people. Traditionally, hymnody has been a proclaiming influence of the things of God. The difficulty with hymns is if they are the only source of song, the triumphant song of God is relegated to a trumpeting of past victory. While hymns fulfill a vital role within the church, they depict foundational understanding and should not serve as the sole voice of musical expression among the people of God.

The Bible speaks of ***pneumatikos*** expressions in conjunction with musical odes in two passages. To the Colossians Paul writes a word on a corporate level, and to the Ephesians he focuses on a personal level. In both instances he gives the same formula of revelation.

> **Colossians 3:16** Let the word of Christ dwell in you richly in all wisdom; teaching and admonishing one another in psalms and hymns and spiritual songs, singing with grace in your hearts to the Lord.

> **Ephesians 5:19** Speaking to yourselves in psalms and hymns and spiritual songs, singing and making melody in your heart to the Lord;

In both of these verses, the procedure begins with an expression of praise to God concerning what He is doing within them at the moment. David's psalms always focused on whatever he was encountering at the time and how that momentary sensation related to the eternal God. If we are not prepared to express thanksgiving and praise to the Lord, we will not proceed through the remaining portion of the creative formula.

After the psalm, Paul focuses on hymnody. This is a reference to the foundational understanding of what God has already done among the people and addresses the cumulative purpose from which those people progress forward in God. Hymns were not to be an end in themselves but a launching and staging vehicle. Hebrews 6 says that we should view foundation as a place from which we build a higher structure.

> **Hebrews 6:1** Therefore leaving the principles of the doctrine of Christ, let us go on unto perfection; not laying again the foundation of repentance from dead works, and of faith toward God,

So, we see that our life should be a continual expression of praise to the Lord. Whatever we encounter, we must convey our feelings in the mode of articulated worship. This can take the shape of varying types of communication, and must be a current enunciation of whatever we are experiencing in God. The personal pursuit of God will augment the corporate, and from that foundational basis God can reveal a creative expression–whether in song or in word.

Before moving into the part of the formula that tells how a mystery is revealed, let us explore the meaning of an *oide*.

THE MEANING OF *OIDE*

An *oide*, or **ode**, is something that depicts a great person or a magnificent occasion of incredible importance. This type of expressive garners fame at the time of creation and gains stature as it spans the course of time. It becomes a battle cry for action and a source of tremendous pride and commemoration. Sometimes these artistic offerings frame the mindset of revolution and invariably become national anthems.

Oide pneumatikos is the type of sound that comes straight from the heart of the Lord. Like the Song of Moses or the Song of the Lamb, it celebrates what God has done and declares His ongoing wonder. Expressions of this magnitude will inspire the people of God in unprecedented fashion.

The type of musician and artist that will birth these songs will consist of part poet, part prophet, total intercessor and faithful lover of God. Humility and devotion will join together as this director and creator of lyric takes strides of faith to birth the song of the Lord. Currently such songs radiate the glory of knowing God. In the future they will also usher in His power and glory in amazing fashion.

Oide pneumatikos will be a declarative weapon on the lips of the saints. The sounds of heaven will emanate from earthly instruments as nations shake in vibrant response. God is currently forming these servants at His feet, and they will burst onto the world scene in the very near future. **Odes** are a type of expression that will prophetically guide the course of God's current move. The **ode** will breathe fervor into the hearts of a waiting people.

THE BIRTHING OF MYSTERY

As the creative formula progresses, we must now link the cited passages of Colossians 3:16 and Ephesians 5:19 with that which is found in 1 Corinthians 14:26.

> **1 Corinthians 14:26** How is it then, brethren? when ye come together, every one of you hath a psalm, hath a doctrine, hath a tongue, hath a revelation, hath an interpretation. Let all things be done unto edifying.

For those who are part of the ***pneumatikos*** church, a prerequisite for coming together is that everyone must have something of spiritual significance with which to contribute. When the Holy Spirit says "everyone," that means you. It also declares that every church should be functioning in this manner.

From this point of initiation, we now juxtapose over ***oide pneumatikos*** these three: tongue, revelation and interpretation. The **ode** is formed by this three-fold pursuit. When we say "tongue" in the context of 1 Corinthians 14, we recognize that it refers to unknown tongues. Psalm and doctrine have already been addressed, so it would be redundant to infer that "tongue" refers to a *koine* expression. Therefore, when we address the subject of unknown tongues, we enter the realm of the currently unknown. How appropriate to consider that for creative purpose we are pursuing the place where we have not been before.

After having acknowledged our entering into the unidentified, we desire to find whatever God is wanting to reveal. Hence, the Spirit provides the word "revelation," or *apokalupsis,* as the next facet of the process. This word means "to take the lid off and look inside;" and in our formula, it easily defines a package of insight that God desires to prophetically reveal and apply.

The final piece of the *oide pneumatikos* formula is interpretation. It is important that interpretation follows revelation and does not follow tongues in this blueprint. Interpretation means an application of what is revealed. Interpretation is what makes prophecy viable and understood.

In typical Pentecostal circles, interpretation is understood to come immediately after the issuance of an unknown tongue. It is usually quick, incisive and painless. When you place interpretation after revelation within the pattern of this passage of scripture, an entirely new concept is discovered. The interpreted application comes after the process of gaining revelation. The middle process of the threefold progression is the meat of the sandwich. It is the most costly and generally the most readily avoided.

This is the task of the *pneumatikos* priesthood:
1. Psalm
2. Hymn or doctrine
3. Tongues
4. Mystery
5. Interpretation

Quite amazingly, this pattern follows the established formula of David throughout the Psalms. He would declare a promise of the Lord and then speak of the challenges that ultimately would be defeated so that the promise would find fulfillment.

THE THREE-FOLD CORD

Ecclesiastes 4:12 ... a threefold cord is not quickly broken.

Truly, the three-fold progression of the revelation that typifies ***pneumatikos*** understanding is nothing new in the scripture. God generally moves in threes, and the sequence is astonishingly the same no matter what God is accomplishing among us. Consider some powerful combinations of three.

Called	Chosen	Faithful
Tongue	Revelation	Interpretation
Chronos (Purpose)	Kairos (Timely Plan)	Promise
Honey Scroll	Bitter Belly	Communicated Message
Mercy Obtained	Process of Finding	Grace
Deliverance	Wilderness	Promised Land
Anointed as King	Hide in Caves	Crowned as King
Born of a Virgin	Death on a Cross	Ascension to Throne
Baptism in Jordan	Wilderness	First Miracle
Death on a Cross	Three Days in Tomb	Resurrection
Righteousness	Peace in Conquest	Joy in the Holy Ghost
Promised Purpose	Selah	Fulfillment

These are only a few of the types of threes that characterize the way God does things in us. In accordance with the theme of ***oide pneumatikos,*** let us consider the concept of the ***selah***. If we really believe that God is establishing the Tabernacle of David in these days, we had better recognize what is meant by the ***selah*** of David's psalms.

Selah is used seventy-four times in the Old Testament: seventy citings in the Psalms and three in Habakkuk. There are five predominate types of ***selahs*** that are typified within these appearances in the Old Testament. These include themes of sacrifice, deliverance, warfare, judgment and triumphant victory. In each instance there is first a need or promise, followed by the *selah,* which leads to provision and culmination of victory.

A *selah* was somewhat of a buffer between a stated promise of God and the fulfillment of that promise. *Selah* was the waiting and travailing between the established need and the answer to that need. It also typified the gap between our sacrifice and the acceptance of our offering. There was no pre-determined, or humanly mandated, time frame for the length of the *selah*. It was simply that the people felt the unction of God and waited upon Him with patience and worship until the acceptance and answer was forthcoming.

The power of the word *selah* has been neutered over the millennia through many influences. Many consider it to represent a simple pause for reflection or a statement of exclamation. The truth of the matter is, when *selah* is mentioned, worshippers are admonished to pour themselves out before God in absolute abandonment recognizing that He is their deliverer and supply. Traditional interpretations of this powerful maxim have removed much of the efficacy of the *selah*.

The *selah* of David's psalms relate perfectly to the revelation process of the *oide pneumatikos* progression which involves waiting upon God. This point of operation is what we are generally unwilling to do on a personal or corporate level. The twenty-four hour a day, seven days per week progression of the Tabernacle of David affords a perfect climate for waiting upon God in such a manner. Regrettably, the one-hour Sunday morning environment does not provide an acceptable climate.

Looking at the larger picture of life, this same three-fold progression applies. Is it not true that God speaks to us about something that He desires, and then there is generally a long period of waiting for that promise to actualize in our lives? This is the three-fold formula of *pneumatikos*.

Unless the church accepts this type of pursuit, we will not know the deep things of God on a continuing basis. Typically the general church is behind the times in the revelation department. The climactic days that are ahead will necessitate our adherence to the necessity of waiting on the Lord.

BATTLE HYMNS

Throughout the recorded history of mankind, song has always played a vital role in defining and forming the mindset of the general public. Contemporary music is the marching cadence of the newest trend and fashionable thought. In warfare each army had a battle song that marked its purpose and inspired the passions of the soldiers within the ranks.

Yankee Doodle, originally a derisive mockery among the British, became the marching ode of the fledgling American patriot. "Dixie" motivated the Southern soldier during the American War Between the States, while the "Battle Hymn of the Republic" was the main anthem of the Union forces. It would seem that every climactic movement of mankind was accompanied by the sound of a prevalent melody and verse.

This is also a vital model within the realm of the spirit. Whenever there is a major shift in the timetable of God, music will also adapt accordingly. It is as if something within the heart of mankind registers the alteration in the territory of the unseen, and song is expressed. Better yet, the forces of good and evil are aware of the power of music in establishing influence within the new climate of existence.

Remarkably, the forces of Satan are more inclined to progressively adapt to new musical style than are the forces of the church. It is tragic that the church is generally willing to employ song only in reference to that which has already been accomplished. Within the framework of the church, the musical expression of yesteryear is staunchly defended as somehow more holy than the new. Perhaps the reason for this is that the people of God do not view themselves as perennial representatives of what God is doing today. Somehow we have been deceived into thinking that the only valid experience with God is the one which earmarked His first move within us. Such thinking dooms us to secondary status and ensures exemption from fresh insight for entire segments of the established church.

The Word of the Lord tells us in Hosea 10:11 that "Judah shall plow, and Jacob shall break his clods." The singers and musicians were placed at the front of God's armies and with good reason. Not only were these worshippers welcoming the hand of the Lord in confident praise, but they were employing the principle of the power of innovative and prophetic song in battle.

The concept of Judah praising is one of incredible significance. With each new move of the Spirit, God must require that we yield all that we have become to the plow of change. God is called a husbandman, and we forget that He must employ the lessons of the best farmers. Before each planting season, the farmer must break up the fields that produced the harvest from the last season. Our iniquities and successes must become the tilled ground for new planting. Only within the church do we enshrine the memory of the previous harvest.

OIDES OF THE PAST GENERATION

In the early 1960's a revolution was getting ready to overtake the world. Spiritual forces were galvanizing for one of the most climactic shifts that the spiritual world has ever experienced. Music began to radically modify in order to fit the anticipation of the moment. Drugs and rock music opened the door into the things of the spirit world, and millions of young people entered in step with the new sound. The United States suffered through the assassination of key leaders, the participation in an unpopular military action in Vietnam, the political unrest and racial tension that erupted on our college campuses and city streets, and a change in every part of our society.

Where was the church during this revolutionary experience? In short, the church was doing what it usually does–not much! The Christian world spent its time preaching about the evils of rock and roll as well as debating the acceptable length of men's hair and women's skirts. The enemy captured the moment in song and spirit while the people of God sat in stunned protest.

One of the reasons that the enemy has been so quick to monopolize on shifts in the timetable of the Lord is that he has long advocated and implemented a group of followers that tap into the things of the spirit. For Satan the concept of the ***pneumatikos*** has long been known. The minions of evil pay a great price to stay current with the most recent trends in the things of the spirit. Jesus declared this aptitude in the gospels.

> **Luke 16:8** And the lord commended the unjust steward, because he had done wisely: for the children of this world are in their generation wiser than the children of light.

It is imperative that the *pneumatikos* become attuned to the sounds of heaven in these days, as a shift in the timetable of God is now visiting us again. Forty years removed from the '60s, God is again moving in a climactic manner. The *pneumatikos* of God will be ready to capitalize during this mighty move, and the results will be far different than those of the '60s and '70s.

The three influences that were utilized by the enemy camp within those tumultuous days were sex, drugs and rock and roll. The *pneumatikos* will focus upon the *agape* of God, prophetic intercession that yields the new wine, and *oide pneumatikos*. God's purpose in the *agape* will show forth intercession in heaven and on earth, and our song and declaration will powerfully explode the realities of God's plan upon this world.

The new sound of the Lord will unlock the hearts of people and will radically change the places where we live. Lyric and melody will powerfully reveal God's arm. God will do a thing in the coming days that will astound everyone, whether saint or sinner.

SUMMATION

> **1 Corinthians 14:1** Follow after charity, and desire spiritual gifts, but rather that ye may prophesy.

Charity, or *agape*, is a devotion to and from our Heavenly Father. From this we receive His revealed directive for ministry. We are shown which areas are to be touched by His hand in the moments immediately ahead. Jesus spoke of this regarding His demonstration of ministry in the Holy Spirit.

> **John 5:19-20** Then answered Jesus and said unto them, Verily, verily, I say unto you, The Son can do nothing of himself, but what he seeth the Father do: for what things soever he doeth, these also doeth the Son likewise. 20 For the Father loveth the Son, and sheweth him all things that himself doeth: and he will shew him greater works than these, that ye may marvel.

As we follow after **charity,** our focus and purpose is clearly exhibited. Within this framework we are told to desire **spiritual** gifts. Literally this verse says that we are to desire *pneumatikos*. Following the Father in *agape* will always flow in tandem with being a proponent of *pneumatikos*. Knowing Him will yield powerful insight and applied wisdom.

As our seeking after God produces insight and maturity, we will then be those who can tangibly speak prophetic words to people and nations. The objective of becoming the *pneumatikos* of God is to please Him in communicating His word and ways to the world. We prophetically minister as priests of the Lord God.

In order to see the Father, we must enter into the realm of the unknown for the purposes of making it known. This is the task of the *pneumatikos*, or priests, of the Father. King David was such a priest. Our Lord Jesus, our Great High Priest, also patterned such behavior. We must adhere to such a walk and devotion if we, too, are to impact our world with the prophetic voice of the Most High.

chapter 9

Pneumatikos Blessings In The Heavenlies

Ephesians 1:3 Blessed be the God and Father of our Lord Jesus Christ, who hath blessed us with all spiritual blessings in heavenly places in Christ:

Whenever we hear the word eulogy, we probably think of a funeral. It has been said that a eulogy will adequately describe what the deceased person should have been rather than what they really had been during their life. How peculiar that God would choose the word *eulogia* to define the manner in which He blesses the *pneumatikos*.

The significance of this is that God sees us through the eyes of what He desires for us. We must become dead to the things of this world in order that the things of God might become our life. When God blesses us, there is a fullness that can only come from Him. Truly, the blessing of the *pneumatikos* is from the Father Himself, and it is complete and timeless.

The book of Ephesians is crucial to our understanding of this type of blessing. God is said to bless us in heavenly places, and this is a phrase that is only found in the writing to the Ephesians.

Heavenly Places

It is imperative to understand that when we speak of the *pneumatikos*, we are unveiling the nature of eternity. In that light, our heavenly blessing has everything to do with what occurs in heavenly places.

Our great High Priest paid the price in order for the ***pneumatikos*** to find their place at the throne of the Father. When He conquered the cross and death, Jesus ascended to this triumphant position. He made possible the place of blessing and commune with the Father.

> **Ephesians 1:20** Which he wrought in Christ, when he raised him from the dead, and set him at his own right hand in the heavenly places.

When we accept Jesus as Savior, we are able to enjoy the prospect of knowing the Father. As we yield ourselves to His plan and demonstrate a willingness to commit our very existence to Him and His ways, we are then permitted access and authority within this place of power and majesty.

> **Ephesians 2:6** And hath raised us up together, and made us sit together in heavenly places in Christ Jesus:

Everything that God does with the ***pneumatikos*** is centered around partnering with Him in accomplishing His plan for the earth. Much of that plan has to do with regaining control of what belongs to Him. With each declared appointment and blessing, God will make certain that the angelic powers of light and darkness are made keenly aware of the legal progression of His will. These transactions and the declaring of them are accomplished from the heavenly places, and God wants all interested parties to be fully apprised.

> **Ephesians 3:10** To the intent that now unto the principalities and powers in heavenly places might be known by the church the manifold wisdom of God,

To then say that God has blessed us with all heavenly blessings entails that we are called to the purpose of ruling and reigning with Christ as sons of God. It also speaks of the purpose of God in reclaiming His footstool.

THE PURPOSE OF GOD

The progression of the blessing of the *pneumatikos* is beautifully outlined within Ephesians 1. Throughout the rest of this chapter, we will primarily focus upon the principles outlined therein.

> **Ephesians 1:9-11** Having made known unto us the mystery of his will, according to his good pleasure which he hath purposed in himself: That in the dispensation of the fulness of times he might gather together in one all things in Christ, both which are in heaven, and which are on earth; even in him: In whom also we have obtained an inheritance, being predestinated according to the

purpose of him who worketh all things after the counsel of his own will:

God's pre-destined purpose (v. 11) was established in Himself (v. 9) before the foundation of the world was made. This purpose is wonderful, and His will includes good pleasure. Hence, what we are doing is beyond our present surroundings. Everything in the *pneumatikos* ministry has to do with God's ultimate purpose for the earth. This is an astounding thought!

Ultimately God desires to do what Jesus taught us to pray: Let the Kingdom of God come and His will be done on earth as it is in heaven. He wants heaven and earth to meet again and for the things of heaven to once more flow mightily upon this earth. God has regulated a systematic progression toward this end, and he has dispensed segments of development in *kairos* moments (v. 10) throughout the ages.

These specific moments on God's timeline, or *kairos* moments, are revealed as mysteries to those who seek the Lord. God uses the word *apokalupsis* to define these mysteries. Literally we are given the privilege of taking the lid off of something that has been preserved and looking in for the purposes of bringing the truth into the world. This is the same word used to define the Revelation of Saint John.

God created this earth to be an outpost of praise and commune with Him, and the very elements of the earth are designed for this purpose. Jesus spoke of the rocks that would cry out in praise if people would not. The trees of the fields clap their hands. Creation groans in anticipation of the ongoing *kairos* manifestations of the sons of God as this signals the increasingly imminent redemption of the planet. Mankind came on the planet long after the foundation of the world was laid. We are a relative newcomer to the scenario, but we are partnering with God in the end of all things – the culmination of the redemption of the earth.

Eden was a small and partial picture of the glorified earth. The rebellious forces of the enemy were still moving freely upon the planet during the tenure of the first Adam. We are not talking about a return to Edenic conditions. What God has in mind predates Eden. God will reveal an existence that is heaven on earth. Again, this is the beginning of the Lord's Prayer. It is ultimately why Jesus came, and it is for this that He continues to intercede. In this context He prays for the saints that they might accomplish the will of the Father.

> **Romans 8:27** And he that searcheth the hearts knoweth what is the mind of the Spirit, because he maketh intercession for the saints according to the will of God.

Ideally the ***pneumatikos*** will ardently pursue the Father for understanding and direction. The saints will flow forth from this climate toward the goal of redeeming the planet from sin and our enemy. This will restore the world unto righteousness. The Antioch pattern of Acts 13 follows this formula as the prophets and teachers prayed and sent forth apostles.

When God first spoke to Abram about righteousness, He linked the concept with the stars of heaven. Continually the stars and righteousness are linked in the Word of God. Essentially God says that the righteous have a responsibility to align the earth with His original creation and design.

> **Psalm 85:6-13** Wilt thou not revive us again: that thy people may rejoice in thee? 7 Shew us thy mercy, O LORD, and grant us thy salvation. 8 I will hear what God the LORD will speak: for he will speak peace unto his people, and to his saints: but let them not turn again to folly. 9 Surely his salvation is nigh them that fear him; that glory may dwell in our land. 10 Mercy and truth are met together; righteousness and peace have kissed each other. 11 Truth shall spring out of the earth; and righteousness shall look down from heaven. 12 Yea, the LORD shall give that which is good; and our land shall yield her increase. 13 Righteousness shall go before him; and shall set us in the way of his steps.

David's words leap off the page as we consider them in their rightful context. God is truly speaking a reviving word to His creation through His saints. The righteous purpose of God looks down from heaven, and the truth of God will spring up out of His earth. ***Penumatikos*** persons are citizens of the heavens that are assigned to an earthly setting. When they partner with the truth of God upon the earth, the righteousness of God will visit from the heavenly places. This is the meaning of the Lord's Prayer when He admonished us to welcome the Kingdom of God to the earth.

> **Psalm 24:1** The earth is the Lord's, and the fulness thereof.

ENLISTING INTO *PNEUMATIKOS*

> **Ephesians 1:4-5** According as he hath chosen us in him before the foundation of the world, that we should be holy and without blame before him in love: Having predestinated us unto the adoption of children by Jesus Christ to himself, according to the good pleasure of his will,

Every person born on the earth has an opportunity to know and flow with the Heavenly Father. We are predestined to adoption as His children (v. 5), and God desires that all would come to the knowledge of Him and His ways. God so loved the world. Toward that end He sent His firstborn Son so that whoever believed in Him might be saved. Jesus did not come to condemn this world but to save it. The continuation of John 3 declares that in this context men and women have the choice of accepting light or darkness, righteousness or unrighteousness.

Predestination means that God has an eternal purpose, and He has a place for everyone within that purpose. Whether they choose to accept that wonderful option is up to them. Those that accept God have a predetermined calling upon their life. In order to activate that calling and move toward being chosen or commissioned as a saint (v. 4), they must access the *agape* of the Father. It is fair to say that God bases everything that He does with mankind on the basis of our relationship with Him. Without a relationship with God, there can be no partnering with Him.

In 1 Corinthians 13 we find that no matter what we do for Him, if we are not motivated for and on behalf of *agape*, it is nothing. *Agape* is the fire of the passion of God burning within us toward the goal of establishing His purpose in and through us. So the commissioning and anointing of the calling is accessed only by virtue of an *agape* relationship with the Father.

Nobody will do this work of righteousness because it is simply a grand idea. This cannot be accomplished by virtue of mental assent and persuasion. No one can accomplish righteousness through philanthropic pursuit, as noble as that may appear. Oh, you may begin the pursuit, but you will not have the staying power because the work of righteousness necessitates a dying to self. Every step taken towards fulfilling purpose is another step closer to killing your ideas and your old nature. Only the *agape* shared between you and your Heavenly Father will bring you to your commissioning.

THE GLORY OF GRACE

Did you know that His grace has glory? Paul says that we should direct praise to God for the glory that is depicted through the demonstration of grace. What in the world does that mean? Simply put, grace is God's manner of promoting and transitioning us from one stage of development to another.

Tragically the only grasp that most believers have concerning grace is that it is amazing or that because of it we are saved from some horrible fate. If not for the hymn "Amazing Grace" or the saying, "There, but for the grace of God, go I," most Christians would not have any association with grace. Subsequently, we relegate grace to the initial and essential work of salvation, but we stop growing right there.

Grace has continuing glory to be able to deliver, promote, and provide whatever we need on the pathway of righteousness. Consider this oft-quoted passage:

2 Corinthians 3:17-4:1 Now the Lord is that Spirit: and where the Spirit of the Lord is, there is liberty. 18 But we all, with open face beholding as in a glass the glory of the Lord, are changed into the same image from glory to glory, even as by the Spirit of the Lord. 4:1 Therefore seeing we have this ministry, as we have received mercy, we faint not;

We have a ministry, and we have received mercy to help us to continue therein. Wherever we obtain mercy, we must also search to find the culmination of grace. God's throne is a throne of grace; and therefore, it dispenses the process of development and promotion.

Hebrews 4:16 Let us therefore come boldly unto the throne of grace, that we may obtain mercy, and find grace to help in time of need.

Ephesians 1:6 To the praise of the glory of his grace, wherein he hath made us accepted in the beloved.

Each time we successfully endure the process of transition and refinement, we find grace and are changed from glory to glory. **Accepted** is the Greek word *charistoo,* which means completed grace. The one that **accepts** and approves us is the **beloved**, or *agape*. This refers to God but also can refer to the *pneumatiko*s and the righteous purpose of God. How wonderfully this flows!

BACK TO THE BEGINNING

> **Ephesians 1:3** Blessed be the God and Father of our Lord Jesus Christ, who hath blessed us with all spiritual blessings in heavenly places in Christ:
>
> **Ephesians 1:11** In whom also we have obtained an inheritance, being predestinated according to the purpose of him who worketh all things after the counsel of his own will:

In light of this, we discover our inheritance (v. 11) and essentially return to Ephesians 1:3 once again. Remember the Bible says in that verse we are blessed with a *pneumatikos* eulogy. This is our life work, and it must be fulfilled.

When Verse 11 refers to heavenly places, it speaks of both our relationship and standing with God at His throne. It declares that we are investing our life in heaven in anticipation of what is coming to earth. Also, it refers us once more to the star-like alignment with righteousness that speaks of God's eternal purpose for His planet.

What a glorious opportunity for the *pneumatikos*, the saints, the general church and the earth. However, we must recognize that there is still an enemy that does not want this triumph to occur. Satan and his minions will contest this righteous plan. The empowering of the Holy Ghost is essential to the victory of the saints. Consider what Jesus said the Holy Spirit would do when the Father sent Him to the earth.

> **John 16:7-13** Nevertheless I tell you the truth; It is expedient for you that I go away: for if I go not away, the Comforter will not come unto you; but if I depart, I will send him unto you. 8 And when he is come, he will reprove the world of sin, and of righteousness, and of judgment: 9 Of sin, because they believe not on me; 10 Of righteousness, because I go to my Father, and ye see me no more; 11 Of judgment, because the prince of this world is judged. 12 I have yet many things to say unto you, but ye cannot bear them now. 13 Howbeit when he, the Spirit of truth, is come, he will guide you into all truth: for he shall not speak of himself; but whatsoever he shall hear, that shall he speak: and he will shew you things to come.

The Holy Ghost will teach the ***pneumatikos*** things that are essential truths for the earth and for the adherence to God's timetable. In this post-resurrection, the Holy Spirit will reprove the world of missing the mark, will declare the righteous purpose of God, and will transact the judgment necessary which affects the coming of His ultimate glory.

chapter 10

Pneumatikos Wickedness In High Places

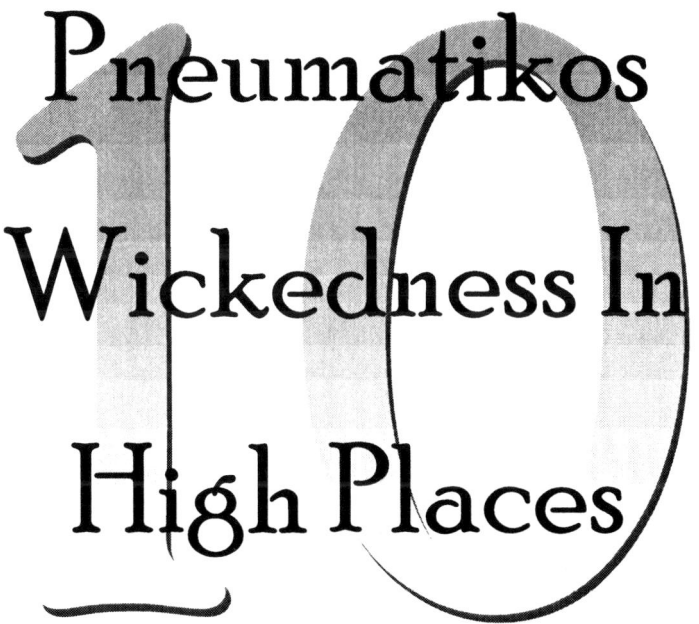

WARFARE IN THE HEAVENS

Ephesians 6:12 For we wrestle not against flesh and blood, but against principalities, against powers, against the rulers of the darkness of this world, against spiritual wickedness in high places.

Embedded in the hierarchy of the enemy realm is *pneumatikos* wickedness in high places. The enemy employs a twisted *pnuematikos* understanding. Even in the Old Testament the kings of Israel were continually warned to tear down the high places in their land. The eventual cause of the downfall of many of them was their disobedience to this directive. The Lord is equipping and giving us instructions to defeat the enemy in the high places. We will be victorious over the expert warriors of the enemy only through recognizing the weapons, insights and relational giftings that God is providing to His church.

We need to know that we will be dealing with demonic individuals in the heavenlies who understand a lot about what we are being given because they were schooled by the Lord when they were flowing in obedience to Him. While they are not privy to the fullness of God's ongoing commune with us, they have enough of an understanding of His ways to be a viable opponent. Add to this the fact they know their time of dominion is short, so they are absolutely devoted to the defense of the things which we are sent to possess.

Five-Fold Opposition To *Pneumatikos*

In a prelude to the challenge to be a *pneumatikos* house, Peter points out five things in direct opposition to moving in the *pnuematikos*.

> **1 Peter 2:1-5** Wherefore laying aside all malice, and all guile, and hypocrisies, and envies, and all evil speaking, 2 As newborn babes, desire the sincere milk of the word, that ye may grow thereby: 3 If so be ye have tasted that the Lord is gracious. 4 To whom coming, as unto a living stone, disallowed indeed of men, but chosen of God, and precious, 5 Ye also, as lively stones, are built up a spiritual house, an holy priesthood, to offer up spiritual sacrifices, acceptable to God by Jesus Christ.

Malice, guile, hypocrisies, envies, and evil speaking are assignments of the enemy that come to stop individuals from going forward in any kind of *pneumatikos* effort. Vestiges of each of these five influences will oppose any *pnuematikos* thrust. Each time the Father gives a new assignment, these five things can be seen over and over again in a similar pattern. Here Peter is warning, "If you are going to be of the *pneumatikos* house, get ready because these five are coming for you." These vile influences are also directly opposed to the five-fold giftings of Christ which are listed in Ephesians 4:11.

MALICE

The Greek word for **malice** is *kakia,* which is a derivative of *kakos*, meaning a depraved, bad, terrible, or maligning influence. *Kakia* is an orchestrating influence that will be assigned with a corps of depraved and terrible messengers of the enemy to attempt to pervert, bring down, corrupt, or cool off the fire. Its influence will attempt to bring a crust around the lively stone that is the heart of the holy priesthood. The end result is that there is still a burning within, but it is completely immobilized and contained.

This directly opposes the apostle. As the Holy Ghost empowers you to go forth, taking possession of locations and allowing victory to be won, the **malice** influence will hit in areas within you that are not yet dead to Christ and will attempt to swing your momentum toward an operation on that level. They lure you to lash out emotionally by accessing iniquity within. When you begin to branch in those directions, you are crusted over and your forward movement is slowed.

This maligning influence will attempt to divert you and get you to fight on the enemy's level. Tauntingly they shout at you,

"Come down out of there, and let us see if you will defend yourself." As God gives you the victory, stay in the victory. Do not come down to the level of soulish or fleshly wisdom as that will allow the enemy to pull you into someplace that you do not belong.

As you begin to move in intercession and offer fiery sacrifices before the Throne of God, you will be confronted by this tactic. Re-entry into the daily environment of your life is when you become vulnerable. The fire will begin to crust over, and you will be burning inside but not really going anywhere.

This happened to Moses. He was at the top of the mountain communing with God at the giving of the Ten Commandments. As Moses returned to the people at the base of the mountain, he faced this influence, and he took the tablets and hurled them down at the people.

Jesus dealt with this same influence when He descended from a mountaintop experience with the Father. It tried to reach Him through His own disciples as He witnessed the undisciplined and ineffective nature of their lives. His response to them was, "How long do I have to be with you, you wicked and perverse generation?" Wicked and perverse things are maligning influences that have not yet been brought into submission to God. We must identify these influences and not give place to them.

The way to defeat this influence is to keep coming up the mountain to the fire of the Lord. The Lord desires for His people to catch on fire, catch cities on fire, and explode before Him as living stones.

GUILE

The maligning influence partners with guile. The Greek word for **guile** is *dolos*, and it means a trick, a wile and a decoy. The maligning influence first analyzes to see how it can get access to you in order to divert you from that lively stone dimension into an area where you can be defeated. He has to trick you to do it.

Guile is the personification of the wiles of the devil. He will bring decoys so that you think that you are acting in accordance with what the Father has sent you to accomplish. This is a misguided assignment in its most deadly form.

The beauty of the office of the evangelist is that God will illuminate strategic strike points into which the explosiveness of the gospel can be inserted. Identifying the crucial point of attack, pursuing the vital juncture of the stronghold, finding the essential position to strike: these are aspects of wisdom that God will pour through the office of the evangelist. Decoy and diversionary measures of guile will attempt to subvert this vital office.

In studying spiritual warfare, we have found that at every boundary of extending the Kingdom of God, the enemy employs a "fifth column" of diversion in an attempt to stay or discourage the advance. Whenever we approach a corridor of conquest, there are generally two opponents: condemnation and mischief.

The mystic realm and much of mythology depicts spiritual beings that specialize in bringing confusion at boundaries. Whenever we have experienced progression into new realms, there is generally a spate of mishaps that occur all around us. These are designed to incur a waste of time, energy and money. People become diverted with necessary duty and many times become very discouraged.

Knowing that this will probably occur is very helpful. No matter how much you might bind and rebuke such happenings, they seem to find some way into your circle. Recognizing that the presence of these influences indicates the advancement of the kingdom instead of defeat can make all the difference to your momentum.

HYPOCRISIES

The next partnering influence is **hypocrisies**, or *hupokrisis*. This word means that a person has made a value judgment or assessment but has made a fatal error in one or more areas of insight. This influence is in direct opposition to the office of the teacher. Accurate information and assessment will defeat this foe.

What is the difference between the preceding influences of **guile** and **hypocrisies**? A hypocrite is somebody who says they are one thing, but they are really something else. **Hypocrisies** flow out of **malice** and **guile**. **Malice** comes and analyzes the situation and brings something that catches your attention. **Guile** tricks you into fighting against this diversion, but you are fighting something that is not a strategic part of the mission of God, a deceit, a feigned thing, and a **hypocrisy**.

In World War II, prior to D-Day, there was an entire staging area that was strategically deployed on the English coast. This great conglomeration of cardboard planes and rubber landing vessels were strategically placed as decoys by the Allied Command. The Germans thought that General Patton was going to be leading one of the main invading thrusts from this location directly across the English Channel. The real invasion came from a totally different location. This effective ruse paralyzed crucial elements of the German occupational forces and lightened opposition in the legitimate invasion landing zones.

The enemy will bring similar "diversions" to distract you by getting you to fight things that have no bearing on your victory. The end result is that you will wear yourself out as well as everyone around you.

ENVIES

Envies are the next partnering influence of five-fold opposition. The Greek word for **envies** is *phonos*, which means ill will or jealousy. This influence pits one against another and directly opposes the office of the pastor. It causes people to be discontent with what they are and to be **envious** of others. Infighting and friendly fire causes the passions within one lively stone to conflict against another lively stone. Since this will affect the pastoral office, every attempt should be made to develop support and supply units in order to keep the leadership unencumbered.

EVIL SPEAKING

The last influence is **evil speaking** and the Greek word is *katalalia,* meaning defamation and backbiting. This is in contrast to *glossalalia,* or speaking in tongues by the words of the Holy Ghost. Defamation, backbiting, friendly fire, and word curses are the enemy's killer blows that hit in strategic and unprotected places. **Evil speaking** tears down, pulls down, and stands in contrast to the prophetic office.

In football, sometimes you will see a running back bust through the line with blazing speed, and one of the linebackers knows he is not going to be able to keep up with him so he dives in an attempt to grab the shirt of the ball carrier. If you are moving forth as a lively stone and something hits you in the back, it will cut off your flow from the source as well as hinder your forward progress.

Speech and declaration are so very powerful in meaning and scope. Jesus referenced the **evil speaking** of the enemy in a very familiar passage.

> **Matthew 5:11-12** Blessed are ye, when men shall revile you, and persecute you, and shall say all manner of evil against you falsely, for my sake. 12 Rejoice, and be exceeding glad: for great is your reward in heaven: for so persecuted they the prophets which were before you.

In this discussion of the attack against the prophetic voice, Jesus refers to the evil that is spoken against them. The word for **evil** in this verse is *rhema*. When we walk in the prophetic realm, we will face strategically placed and effective words that will be launched against us from enemy forces. While these words are part of the arsenal of our enemy, the Lord gives a solution for them. We need to be exceeding glad and rejoice in view of what we are accomplishing for the Father. Jesus endured the cross because of His love for the Father and in the face of the joy that was set before Him.

Evil speaking will come against you. Knowing this, reacting appropriately and not becoming a vessel of such speech is essential to overcoming.

Peter's Experiences

On one occasion Peter received insight from the Father to the degree that he declared, "You are the Christ, the son of the living God." Jesus replied, "Peter, flesh and blood did not reveal this to you but My Father which is in heaven has given it to you." Then Peter proceeded to rebuke the purpose of the Father by saying, "Now, Lord, think about this. You do not need to go and die in Jerusalem. We have swords and we will fight." Jesus said, "Get thee behind me, Satan."

Peter had spiritual interference that clouded his revelation, but he also had personal experience of yielding to evil speaking during times of duress. Immediately prior to the cross, before the cock crowed three times, he was speaking out evil words of defamation, curse words, and denial of the Lord. The maligning influence came to Peter and began to touch him.

What would it touch in Peter? In the flesh, the brash Peter wanted to win. He desired to have the kingdom established, not to have the King killed. So he was open for deception and summarily was tricked and wiled. He began to declare something different than the Lord's words. Hypocrisy crept in, "Master, you could be a survivor instead of what you have taught over and over again. Just let us fight and win instead."

Peter understood this process because he saw it happen over and over again in himself and the other disciples. These same influences were working double time on another disciple named Judas who ended up betraying the Lord.

LAYING ASIDE

Now, what does Peter say about these five things? Does he say we fight them until we win? Does he say we study them until we know all there is to know so we can outsmart them? Does he say we make declarations against them? No, he clearly says we lay them aside.

We know they are coming, so when we see them, we need to just lay them aside. So what does that mean? Returning to the same football illustration, if a running back is carrying the ball and a defensive player comes to stop him, the best thing he can do is strong arm him and put him aside. Even the sculpture on the Heisman Trophy depicts the effectiveness of this maneuver. If the running back were to stop and begin fighting him, it would not accomplish anything but a penalty. Laying aside means to stay above it, to walk around or over it.

AS NEWBORN BABES

Peter warned of the five influences to watch out for and then immediately said, "As newborn babes desire the sincere milk of the word that you may grow thereby." The operative phrasing here is "as newborn babes." If you have ever been around a newborn babe, what is the one thing they want the most? They want to be as close to the nurturer as possible.

Our best strategy for defense against five-fold opposition to *pneumatikos* is to stay as close to our Nurturer as we possibly can. Our Heavenly Father is our source and supply. We draw life from Him. The way to overcome the attack of the enemy is to keep going back to the Father, to be undaunted in our pursuit of the Father, and to just tap into Him. This is the only way to defuse malice. If we allow ourselves to lose sight of our first love, we become as the

Ephesian church. They were made famous for their grasp of the incredible insights into the Kingdom of God as well as for becoming diverted from their first love toward the Heavenly Father.

We can very easily become distracted by the deceitful tricks and wiles of the enemy. These will generally focus upon the unrefined aspects of our nature and the iniquity within that has yet to be corrected. We then channel our passion toward the defense of ourselves instead of the pursuit of our God. Suspicion, ill will, jealousy, backbiting, and defamation of our brethren will all come flooding into our being. In this way the enemy cuts us off from our true source.

> **Galatians 5:14-18** ... Thou shalt love thy neighbour as thyself. 15 But if ye bite and devour one another, take heed that ye be not consumed one of another. 16 This I say then, Walk in the Spirit, and ye shall not fulfil the lust of the flesh. 17 For the flesh lusteth against the Spirit, and the Spirit against the flesh: and these are contrary the one to the other: so that ye cannot do the things that ye would. 18 But if ye be led of the Spirit, ye are not under the law.

SAFETY IN HIGH PLACES

We have been given our place of dominion and authority as we are seated in heavenly places in Christ Jesus. God has given His directives to us, and we are assigned to carry them out in the place that we have been planted. The enemy will attempt to subvert our adherence to this entire progression. We must remain oblivious to his movements, reckoning ourselves dead to this world and its passions. We have been called to exist far above all of the forces of the enemy. Our devotion should be to remain in absolute alignment with the plans and purposes of our Heavenly Father.

Pneumatikos

chapter 11

On Earth As It Is In Heaven

Partnering With The Host Of The Lord

Many times within this book, as well as within the companion volume entitled **The Saints**, we see the partnership that God created between His servants and the angels. An incredible study of this topic can be found in the book entitled **Ministering With Angels** by my friend Paul David Harrison. For the purposes of this writing, it is vital that we ascertain the objectives that require the partnering between God's angels, the *pneumatikos* and the saints.

God created Adam for the purpose of communing with Him. He also desired that Adam become a partner with Him in transacting the business of this earth. God sent His Son to die in order that mankind might enjoy these privileges once again. The Heavenly Father is looking for sons who will work with Him in the family business. The process of developing these sons is the topic of this book and of **The Saints**.

Sons Of God In Heaven

It is my opinion, based upon a preponderance of scripture, that the sons of God are comprised of a grouping of ruling forces within the heavens. When Satan fell, and the rebellion of some of the angels occurred, vacancies were created within this structure.

In the life of Job this grouping of ruling forces was convened within the courts of heaven. It was to this place that Satan came to accuse Job.

> **Job 1:6-7** Now there was a day when the sons of God came to present themselves before the Lord, and Satan came also among them. 7 And the Lord said unto Satan, Whence comest thou? Then Satan answered the Lord, and said, From going to and fro in the earth, and from walking up and down in it.

The Bible tells us that the enemy roams about seeking what he may devour. He did this in the days of Job, and he continues to do so now. He returns to this gathering of the sons of God on a regular basis in order to accuse the brethren.

Originally the sons of God had responsibilities upon the earth that were incredibly important. When the rebellion of Satan occurred, many of these sons fell with him. It is these places that God has called the saints to take back in violent fashion. In the days of Noah, some of these fallen sons desired to take an active role on the earth once again. They acted in depravity and in direct disobedience to the purpose of God for populating the earth.

> **Genesis 6:1-3** And it came to pass, when men began to multiply on the face of the earth, and daughters were born unto them, 2 That the sons of God saw the daughters of men that they were fair; and they took them wives of all which they chose.

These sons of God were punished and immediately removed from their place of estate, or rulership, and imprisoned until the time of the end.

> **Jude 1:6** And the angels which kept not their first estate, but left their own habitation, he hath reserved in everlasting chains under darkness unto the judgment of the great day.

Once again, it is God's plan that the faithful angels and redeemed man partner together with Him for the purposes of redeeming the earth from the current prince of this world. There are many places on earth and in the heavenlies that are still inhabited by the fallen angels that were originally created to rule therein. God wants His redeemed sons to partner with Him in restoring His creation to its original purpose.

When John the Baptist began to minister before the Lord, this process of kingdom taking began in earnest. This is the New Covenant in all of its splendor and is a true depiction of the will and kingdom of God coming to earth as it is in heaven.

Matthew 11:12 And from the days of John the Baptist until now the kingdom of heaven suffereth violence, and the violent take it by force.

Remember that the concept described here involves a forcing out of one occupying force by virtue of a greater force coming into power. This is a wrestling match of strategy, position and endurance.

Much of this process is by faith and requires a commitment on behalf of the sons that is not currently rewarded in physical manifestation. John wrote of this in his first Epistle.

1 John 3:2 Beloved, now are we the sons of God, and it doth not yet appear what we shall be: but we know that, when he shall appear, we shall be like him; for we shall see him as he is.

Obviously the sons of God are the redeemed individuals that have exercised the "power to become" the things that Jesus patterned.

SEATED

In the letter to the Ephesian church, Paul speaks of our being seated in heavenly places, far above all of the enemy chain of command. By reason of the triumph of Jesus, we are permitted the privilege of sharing this place, this dominion and this relationship with the Father. The seats are positions of power and authority in service to the Heavenly Father.

> **Ephesians 2:6** And hath raised us up together, and made us sit together in heavenly places in Christ Jesus:

The location of these seats is a very real and operational setting. I have had the honor of walking and interceding within this corridor and transacting business before the throne of grace. These twenty-four seats are dedicated to the service of the King and are designed to oversee and transact kingdom business. There is great interaction and cooperation between each of these sectors. Saints and elders, both contemporary and eternal, comprise the makeup of this ruling body.

When the church that I pastor accepted our calling to be an intercessory church, our only motive was to seek after the heart of our Heavenly Father. Angelic activity was prevalent, and many visual depictions of the spirit realm were evident during our times of prayer. On one particular occasion, I perceived that our sanctuary was actually enveloped by another much grander backdrop. After several occasions of witnessing this magnificent occurrence, I recognized that we were participating in something that was much larger than our small church.

On a day that I will never forget, two angelic messengers told me to prepare for an audience with the Father. I proceeded to the balcony of our church and was immediately seated in a large chair in a setting that was no longer of this earth. Moving about in front of me was a dark specter, and the caustic intent of this being was to discredit me. Every word that was spoken penetrated into me like a flaming sword. Finally, after what seemed like an eternity, I appealed to the Lord for His mercy. Suddenly the Lord Jesus came from the right and silenced the enemy. The Lord smiled at me and stretched forth His hand toward my heart, and I was immediately back in the confines of the balcony of our church. From that day on I was convinced that we were seated in the heavenlies as we interceded before the Lord God.

Although I am not visually aware of this area every time I pray, it is important to remember that my conversation is always in heaven. Even from the most elementary level of commune with God, we must realize the fact that God is always with us and that we belong to Him. In the deeper things of His Spirit, it is imperative to know our place in Him.[3]

---

[3] For a closer look at this topic, obtain **Ministering From Our Heavenly Seats** by Paul David Harrison, Pneumatikos Publishing

> **Philippians 3:20** For our conversation is in heaven; from whence also we look for the Saviour, the Lord Jesus Christ.

Where Do You Live?

The writer to the Hebrews tells us that the church must recognize its place in God. When we become a part of God's family, we experience a bit of what Jacob did as he gained favor with God and man (Genesis 32:32). Like Jacob, God desires that we live in this way and cease operating according to our own devices. Jacob was continually met by angels and constantly surrounded by the presence of the heavenly host.

> **Genesis 32:2** And when Jacob saw them, he said, This is God's host: and he called the name of that place Mahanaim.

Mahanaim means the place of the double camp. At this time you are living in a physical body but are surrounded by the presence of God. Things are transpiring in your spiritual surroundings that are more real than that which you behold with your physical eyes. God tells us in His Word that we must continually live in this wisdom.

> **2 Corinthians 4:18** While we look not at the things which are seen, but at the things which are not seen: for the things which are seen are

temporal; but the things which are not seen are eternal.

It is imperative that we recognize this fact and begin to live our lives accordingly. Our home is in the heavens! Not only in the sweet bye and bye, but NOW!

> **Hebrews 12:22-24** But ye are come unto mount Sion, and unto the city of the living God, the heavenly Jerusalem, and to an innumerable company of angels, 23 To the general assembly and church of the firstborn, which are written in heaven, and to God the Judge of all, and to the spirits of just men made perfect, 24 And to Jesus the mediator of the new covenant, and to the blood of sprinkling, that speaketh better things than that of Abel.

The heavenly Mount Zion is a wondrous place! It is the place where God interacts with His creation in rejoicing and delight. It is characterized in scripture as being "the sides of the north" and is where the congregation meets to worship and rejoice in the midst of God's splendor. The enemy hates this place and desires to possess the power of such grandeur and adoration.

> **Isaiah 14:13** For thou hast said in thine heart, I will ascend into heaven, I will exalt my throne above the stars of God: I will sit also upon the mount of the congregation, in the sides of the north:

Not only does the enemy lust after this powerful and compelling position of passionate exchange, he longs to keep the believer from participating in this atmosphere. While he has not been able to overcome the throne of God, he has been largely successful in keeping the believer from participating in the pleasures of communing in Zion.

All believers have the privilege of enjoying this environment, but the saints are imperatively involved within this Holy Mount. When we fellowship with the Lord, we are welcomed into Zion. What a confident and joyful environment! God's Word says that He loves the gates of Zion. Why would we not desire to meet Him at that place of commune?

THE SIDES OF THE NORTH

Many descriptions of the heavens are reliant upon the subjective nature of our individual interpretation. This is why so many who have shared visions or dreams of the heavens are often seemingly contradictory in their depictions. Like anything else in life, any two witnesses of the same event will report varying definitions of what actually transpired. No person will ever be able to define all of the wonders of this glorious place, but some aspects of our heavenly home are constant for all to see.

The eastern fringes of the sides of the north extend as a greeting place for newcomers. Like a Grand Central Station of Heaven, it is the general connective between heaven and earth. There is much delight as believers go from this life into eternity. The tree of life and the river of life flow freely from the Mount of God through this area. As a result of this source of life, there is vibrant and colorful foliage of resplendent variety.

It is in this section of heaven that believers who have died, will be led into heaven. They will enter through a cloud-like veil and at that point will be changed into their eternal body. The Lord has allowed me to witness this transformation on two occasions. This is the juncture of receiving and participating in eternity.

God says that when we come to our Mount Zion, we are surrounded by the magnificent gathering detailed in Hebrews 12. This will occur when the believer passes from this life to the next, but it should be recognized every time we come together as a church. It should be appreciated every moment of our lives. We are "of" that world, not the one in which we temporarily exist.

BEASTS, ELDERS AND SAINTS

Revelation 5:8-11 And when he had taken the book, the four beasts and four and twenty elders

> fell down before the Lamb, having every one of them harps, and golden vials full of odours, which are the prayers of saints. 9 And they sung a new song, saying, Thou art worthy to take the book, and to open the seals thereof: for thou wast slain, and hast redeemed us to God by thy blood out of every kindred, and tongue, and people, and nation; 10 And hast made us unto our God kings and priests: and we shall reign on the earth. 11 And I beheld, and I heard the voice of many angels round about the throne and the beasts and the elders: and the number of them was ten thousand times ten thousand, and thousands of thousands;

The creatures identified as the four beasts work closely with the twenty-four elders in accomplishing the work of God. The four beasts are exceptional in beauty and are entrusted with the privilege of overseeing the ways of God throughout the heavens and on the earth.

The twenty-four elders are individuals that have been redeemed by the blood of the Lamb. The identity of these individuals is shown forth by the fact that they have been recruited from every people group. They are in the saints/***pneumatikos*** class, as they are priests and kings that rule on the earth on God's behalf. They each possess a musical instrument which can only mean that they are familiar with songs of creative worship and warfare. The vials infer that they are also a communing and interceding group.

Theologians have defined the elders in ways that are incredibly vague. The elders have been designated as "heavenly senators" as well as many other aliases. The fact of the matter is that these individuals are redeemed people that have served God in meritorious ways. They serve more as kings than as senators. God has promoted them and empowers them now to transact His bidding on behalf of this world. Since they were redeemed by the blood of the Lamb of God, they are aligned with the purposes of those saints who still labor in their human existence upon the earth.

The elders are a humble group and do not flaunt their rank or authority. Truly, the greatest of all are most readily portrayed as servants. For that matter, there is no pomp or pretense among any of the redeemed or angelic. Everyone is devoted to the service of the Most High, and they are committed to their assigned duty and responsibility. Interacting and cooperating with each other for the benefit of the King is a privilege.

There have been many times that I have recognized people groups of various nationalities. Often within the framework of intercession at our church, we have experienced languages of the nations on earth and have partnered in the realm of vision with other intercessory groups in prayer. With regularity I see and interact with some of the same leaders over and over again. These rulers seem to coordinate and supervise the seats of the sons of God.

WHERE THE ELDERS MEET

The throne of God is always due north. God's eminence and magnificent presence adorn this place of His throne. Nothing can compare to the majesty of this heavenscape. Like the differences between the salvation experiences of born-again individuals, no two gatherings unto God are alike.

The place where the sons of God convene is close to the throne of God. It is a place of business, and the strategies of the saints are conveyed therein. The appearance seems to embody both a sense of vastness and imminence. There are times when the floor seems crystal-clear and other times when it appears to be filled with fire. Often one is made aware of the presence of great multitudes of devoted individuals. At times you feel absolutely alone with God. Entering into this place is incredible in that you recognize that the Heavenly Father has chosen to summon you to Him, when at the same time He is also able to transact a myriad number of other duties. What an incredible Father.

The configuration of the twenty-four thrones is circular, but each chair seems to be equidistant to God. We are there because of

Jesus, and His omnipresence takes on an intimate quality in this environment as each representative has an equal share and attention from the Lord. His intercession on behalf of the saints is no more evident than here in this place. He stands with you and oversees each detail of your life and purpose.

Within the transaction of intercessory business, one often becomes aware of the presence of others. Although the only authority that really stands out is that of Jesus Himself. He is the KING of KINGS, representing the elders. He is also the LORD of LORDS, depicted by the myriad number of saints that flow within the assignments from the Father. In all there is an absolute humility as Jesus is the only one that matters.

Aligned with each throne there is an antechamber that directly correlates with the business of the chair itself. Like the very chambers of the heart of God, these places of commune roughly pattern those which were displayed within the Old Testament temple.

Within these places, commune with God takes place concerning His purpose that is being transacted upon the earth and in the heavens. Herein is a place of love, instruction and training before our Heavenly Father.

Knowing God's Ways

Above all other things, every saint is going to be an intercessor. This is the life breath of the saintly calling. Look at the manner in which the prayers of the saints are regarded by the angels.

> **Revelation 8:4-6** And the smoke of the incense, which came with the prayers of the saints, ascended up before God out of the angel's hand. 5 And the angel took the censer, and filled it with fire of the altar, and cast it into the earth: and there were voices, and thunderings, and lightnings, and an earthquake. 6 And the seven angels which had the seven trumpets prepared themselves to sound.

It would seem that everything that God does begins with a voice. Wherever you look in the Bible, God always initiates His works with a spoken word, whether through Him or through one of His appointed servants. One of the blessings of flowing in *pneumatikos* understanding is that we have the privilege of understanding the ways of God.

The angels respond to this progression, as if it were a cardinal rule of heaven, a formula that is followed throughout creation. This formula begins with voices, and this is why God loves His intercessors so very much. They just cannot help but talk with Him. Before He does anything, the Bible says that He speaks of it to His friends who will prophesy, or speak it forth. Voices are essential to whatever God is doing.

Thunders follow and indicate a change of atmosphere or climate. When the voices reach their intended culmination regarding the purpose of God, thunderings indicate a changing of the conditions that have been addressed. Sometimes there is an audible thundering, and at other times there is simply an adjustment of the controlling pressures of a realm or circumstance. Thunder signifies change. Lightning is a direct expression of the enforcement of the colliding of atmospheres. God chooses lightning as a major weapon within His arsenal, and it is one in which He demonstrates His power and brilliant light to transact His command and intent.

The four-phased course of action concludes with earthquakes or shakings which speaks of a lasting change in the physical makeup of things. Shakings are foretold for the changing of the earth and of the heavens. The writer to the Hebrews shares a powerful prophetic insight regarding a coming depiction of this progression.

> **Hebrews 12:25-27** See that ye refuse not him that speaketh. For if they escaped not who refused him that spake on earth, much more shall not we escape, if we turn away from him that speaketh from heaven: 26 Whose voice then shook the earth: but now he hath promised, saying, Yet once

> more I shake not the earth only, but also heaven. 27 And this word, Yet once more, signifieth the removing of those things that are shaken, as of things that are made, that those things which cannot be shaken may remain.

The voices of intercessors merge with the voices of those that serve God in heaven. Ultimately, God's voice has prompted them. Just as His voice created all things, that same voice will draw all things into alignment once again. We are living in that day. Atmospheres in the spirit realm are changing, and the days of lightning and shakings are upon us. Signs in the heavens and in the earth beneath are beginning to be seen. What a glorious hour to live for the King and to be His servants!

Voices are essential, and like Daniel of old, intercession is necessary for all of the purposes of God to transpire. God must have a people to partner with, and the Bible says that He searches for intercessors to stand for Him where nobody else will. In that light, a gap in intercessions is where the enemy will pour through the line. Intercessors stand against the movements and intent of the enemy who would plunge through the hedge. These intercessors fill the gap between heaven and earth, ensuring a continuity of the flow of God's purpose

.

chapter 12

The church that is alive today is going to see the hand of God in ways that have never been seen before. God is literally going to take this planet, and all of His creation, unto Himself. The jealousy of God demands a returning of what belongs to Him as well as an alignment with His purpose.

> **Isaiah 42:13-15** The Lord shall go forth as a mighty man, he shall stir up jealousy like a man of war: he shall cry, yea, roar; he shall prevail against his enemies. 14 I have long time holden my peace; I have been still, and refrained myself: now will I cry like a travailing woman; I will destroy and devour at once. 15 I will make waste mountains and hills, and dry up all their herbs; and I will make the rivers islands, and I will dry up the pools.

God has held His peace for a very long time; but when He speaks, it will not be a whisper. God says that He will cry and roar. Our Father has been training His servants to intercede in such a travailing manner.

THE CULMINATION OF KINGDOM TAKING

When we read in Daniel, we find that the evil rulers of the end times will be mightily opposed by the saints of God. These mighty men and women will be a force for the purposes of God all over the planet. Signs, wonders, and many miracles will occur in the war against darkness. Apparently these individuals will be paired in twos, just as the Lord sent forth His disciples.

One such pair is known as the two witnesses, or two that are willing to die. This word for witnesses is the same that is translated as "witness" in the Temple of the Tabernacle of witness in heaven. Traditional interpretation as to the identity of this pair will suppose them to be Moses and Elijah. It makes much more sense to assume that these are the last two of the mighty ones that are left on the earth during the tribulation.

> **Revelation 11:3-8** And I will give power unto my two witnesses, and they shall prophesy a thousand two hundred and threescore days, clothed in sackcloth. 4 These are the two olive trees, and the two candlesticks standing before the God of the earth. 5 And if any man will hurt them, fire proceedeth out of their mouth, and devoureth their enemies: and if any man will hurt them, he must in this manner be killed. 6 These have power to shut heaven, that it rain not in the days of their prophecy: and have power over waters to turn them to blood, and to smite the earth with all plagues, as often as they will. 7 And when they shall have finished their testimony, the beast that ascendeth out of the bottomless pit shall make war against them, and shall overcome them, and kill them. 8 And their dead bodies shall lie in the street of the great city, which spiritually is called Sodom and Egypt, where also our Lord was crucified.

The Lord accomplishes through their martyrdom a cleansing of the most vital of earthly sites, that being Jerusalem. The forerunner ministry that was begun by John the Baptist has now reached its appointed climax. Jesus said that John began the process of redeeming the Kingdom in Matthew 11:12.

When these remaining two witnesses are martyred, they complete the chain of acquisition that was begun by John. According to the passage that follows, these two individuals are miraculously raised from the dead. The earth experiences a mighty wrenching as the hand of God grasps His footstool. In heaven the pronouncement is made that the kingdoms of the world are now legally in the possession of the Most High.

> **Revelation 11:11-15** And after three days and an half the Spirit of life from God entered into them, and they stood upon their feet; and great fear fell upon them which saw them. 12 And they heard a great voice from heaven saying unto them, Come up hither. And they ascended up to heaven in a cloud; and their enemies beheld them. 13 And the same hour was there a great earthquake, and the tenth part of the city fell, and in the earthquake were slain of men seven thousand: and the remnant were affrighted, and gave glory to the God of heaven. 14 The second woe is past; and, behold, the third woe cometh quickly. 15 And the seventh angel sounded; and there were great voices in heaven, saying, The kingdoms of this world are become the kingdoms

of our Lord, and of his Christ; and he shall reign for ever and ever.

These events signal the beginning of what the Word says is the third woe. This signifies the beginning of the final phase of God's purging process.

THE SEVEN ANGELS

In Revelation 15 the seven angels are the bearers of the seven last plagues that are to be released upon the earth. This is undoubtedly a part of the third woe that is spoken of in Revelation 11.

> **Revelation 15:1-4** And I saw another sign in heaven, great and marvellous, seven angels having the seven last plagues; for in them is filled up the wrath of God. 2 And I saw as it were a sea of glass mingled with fire: and them that had gotten the victory over the beast, and over his image, and over his mark, and over the number of his name, stand on the sea of glass, having the harps of God. 3 And they sing the song of Moses the servant of God, and the song of the Lamb, saying, Great and marvellous are thy works, Lord God Almighty; just and true are thy ways, thou King of saints. 4 Who shall not fear thee, O Lord, and glorify thy name? for thou only art holy: for all nations shall come and worship before thee; for thy judgments are made manifest.

The grouping of seven angels occurs in many instances within the Book of Revelation. They are continually in partnership with the saints in the subjugation of the earth in accordance with the purpose of God.

The King of Saints is triumphantly praised as His redeemed forces proclaim Him in glorious ***oides*** on behalf of His great victories. Currently these seven mighty angels are involved in the preparation and training of the saints and ***pneumatikos***. Within this instruction there is tremendous significance in the song of Moses and the Lamb.

Jesus as King presides over a people that are desirous of declaring God's ways and that are willing to become agents of obedient deliverance from the power of darkness. The song of these redeemed and victorious ones will radiate the virtues of the finger of God. His mighty ways will be established, and the kingdom of darkness will be pushed back.

MOSES AND THE LAMB

We are very familiar with Moses, the lawgiver. He led the people of God out of bondage toward a bright promised land. Moses was a friend of God, and he strove to know the ways of the Almighty. Our Lord Jesus bridged the gap between law and grace.

He became the doorway to the Father through His sacrifice at Calvary.

Both Moses and Jesus yielded themselves so that others might enjoy their victory. Moses deferred his mantle to Joshua. Jesus made the way for us to do greater works than He.

> **John 1:12** But many as received Him, to them gave He the power to become the sons of God...

These men had two other things in common.

THE FINGER OF GOD IN THE MINISTRY OF MOSES AND JESUS

The finger of God in the Bible is isolated to the life and ministries of Moses and Jesus. Moses witnessed the finger of God in the delivery of the law on the mountain.

> **Exodus 31:18** And he gave unto Moses, when he had made an end of communing with him upon mount Sinai, two tables of testimony, tables of stone, written with the finger of God.

Jesus demonstrated the finger of God in the power of deliverance from demonic possession. In this ministry He depicted dominance over the binding forces of Beelzebub.

> **Luke 11:20** But if I with the finger of God cast out devils, no doubt the kingdom of God is come upon you.

Matthew identifies this finger as being the Spirit of God. The end result is the same in both parallel passages, as the power of demonic gives way to the hand of God.

Moses and Jesus depict the finger of God as the foundational truths for mankind that provide freedom and deliverance.

THE WORDS OF MALACHI 4

Within the last words of the Old Covenant, Malachi links the works of the Lord Jesus with that of Moses.

> **Malachi 4:2-6** But unto you that fear my name shall the Sun of righteousness arise with healing in his wings; and ye shall go forth, and grow up as calves of the stall. 3 And ye shall tread down the wicked; for they shall be ashes under the soles of your feet in the day that I shall do this, saith the Lord of hosts. 4 Remember ye the law of Moses my servant, which I commanded unto him in Horeb for all Israel, with the statutes and judgments. 5 Behold, I will send you Elijah the prophet before the coming of the great and dreadful day of the Lord: 6 And he shall turn the heart of the fathers to the children, and the heart of the children to their fathers, lest I come and smite the earth with a curse.

This prolific passage proclaims that righteousness, or God's purpose, will be revealed from the east. His glory will be depicted from the rising of a new day. Healing and deliverance will penetrate the darkness as the rays of righteousness stretch across the land. This power progression will build upon a remembrance of the law of Moses but will find its prominence in the ministry of the Lord Jesus. John the Baptist is the next prophet to grace the pages of the Word of God, and our Lord Jesus identifies him as being representative of Elijah.

> **Matthew 17:11** And Jesus answered and said unto them, Elias truly shall first come, and restore all things.

To restore means to establish something that should be in place within the realm to which it is sent. This is an apostolic sending forth of the plan of God for the hour. Obviously John the Baptist and Elijah prepared the way just as Moses and Jesus prepared the way of righteousness for others.

So in this respect the song of Moses and the Lamb are worshipful expressions of those that went forth as point men to declare the righteous ways of the Lord. These mighty ones of God went forth before it was popular to do so and established the way of righteousness. They are first fruits of the ways of God in the last days.

The Temple Of The Tabernacle Of Testimony

The continuation of Revelation 15 provides many incredible insights concerning the priests of the Lord.

> **Revelation 15:5-8** And after that I looked, and, behold, the temple of the tabernacle of the testimony in heaven was opened: 6 And the seven angels came out of the temple, having the seven plagues, clothed in pure and white linen, and having their breasts girded with golden girdles. 7 And one of the four beasts gave unto the seven angels seven golden vials full of the wrath of God, who liveth for ever and ever. 8 And the temple was filled with smoke from the glory of God, and from his power; and no man was able to enter into the temple, till the seven plagues of the seven angels were fulfilled.

The temple of the tabernacle of testimony is a very real place in heaven. It is adjacent to the area that houses the Throne of God, and it is a location that is vital to the transaction of the purposes of God through the saints and angels.

We must consider the implications of this temple. Every saintly intercessor has a place within this temple. It is their interaction with the Father that sends the seven angels on their appointed duties.

Many of you that are reading this book have already been privileged to access this temple. Ezekiel and David were given a description of the beauties of this glorious structure. Within the corridors of this place, the tabernacle of David abides.

The entry point of this place is your very life, as the tabernacle of testimony is a tabernacle of death to the world. One of the powerful meanings of the Greek word for testimony is that it is utilized in Acts 1:8 to define the witnesses that will flow in the power of the Holy Ghost. To operate in the promised power of Pentecost, we must be willing to lay down our life for the service of the Spirit of God. These *marturion* are willing to sacrifice all that they are in order for God's will to be conducted through them.

We witness this powerful theme in the description of the earthly Temple that was constructed by Solomon through the heavenly vision of his father David.

> **1 Kings 7:21** And he set up the pillars in the porch of the temple: and he set up the right pillar, and called the name thereof Jachin: and he set up the left pillar, and he called the name thereof Boaz.

Note the two pillars in the porch of the temple. The right pillar was named Jachin, which means established. To the left was Boaz, meaning strength and alacrity. A quick study of left and right in the Bible will help us to ascertain why this nomenclature is significant for us in following the purposes of God.

Many believers will readily accept what is represented by the right hand, as it establishes the prophetic vision within people. There are scores of folk that will agree to what God wants, and perhaps they will even get excited about the prospects of what is depicted prophetically. When it comes to the *selah* that extends between the promise and the fulfillment, they balk.

Those that desire quick fulfillment without honoring the cost are doomed to failure. The Bible provides many instances of the folly of focusing only on easy gratification, typified by a premature spotlight on the left. The men of Benjamin were left-handed, and they welcomed Belial into their midst. King Saul flowed out of this tribe that was almost destroyed because of their toleration of the left. A New Testament man named Sceva, whose name means left, had seven sons that wanted to execute deliverance from the demonic without a relationship born of devotion to God. Their view of perfect timing was not God's view, and they suffered the consequence of defeat. Lot chose the left, which was the easy life of Sodom and Gomorrah, and Abraham chose the right. In the coming day of judgment, God will preserve His sheep on the right, and the goats of the left will be destroyed.

Proverbs 3:16 says that the right hand may encompass many days. When those days have been accomplished, there will be riches and honor in the left. God's suddenly of visitation will come upon those that wait upon the prophetic vision. Only those that are devoted to receiving the prophetic word of the Lord and commit themselves to the fulfillment of His timing will be permitted to enter and operate within this heavenly temple. God identifies Himself as Yea and Amen, Alpha and Omega, Author and Finisher, Beginning and Ending. The "and" within those titles is where most believers fall short of completion in the purposes of God.

Our Lord tells us that when we are offering ourselves to Him in service, we should concentrate on what it is that He is requiring of us. If we are in the right side of prophetic activation, we should not become overly interested in when the fulfillment of the promise should come. Whether we are laboring with the prospect of authoring or finishing, we must be content to serve Him with all of our energies.

> **Matthew 6:3-4** But when thou doest alms, let not thy left hand know what thy right hand doeth: 4 That thine alms may be in secret: and thy Father which seeth in secret himself shall reward thee openly.

Those that enter into this temple must commit to the fullness of God's purpose and plan. They must not become concerned about the "when of God" in their life or in the lives of others. Within the

Revelation of John, the saints are said to be patient and faithful. These are the keys that activate entry into the temple of the Most High.

chapter 13

Perhaps the wisest manner in which to conclude this writing is simply to provide a picture of the way things will transpire at the very end. We find this in the twentieth chapter of the Book of Revelation.

> **Revelation 20:9** And they went up on the breadth of the earth, and compassed the camp of the saints about, and the beloved city: and fire came down from God out of heaven, and devoured them.

Incredible warfare will transpire between the forces of God and of the world. This conflict will affect the church in the same manner that war always influences a people. Some will rise to become heroes for the cause, others will fearfully do their duty, while others will offer anything in the way of appeasement or surrender in order to preserve their own life. Sometimes, the only thing that will separate the hero from the coward is that the hero chooses to hold on for just a little bit longer before giving up.

Our best maxim for survival is to commit ourselves to death right now. Jesus came to earth to die. When you think of it, every person born upon this planet is born to die. The cemeteries are filled with indispensable people. So, it is not a matter of if you will die, but a matter of how and when. It would be better to purpose to die to the world and yourself and to do it right now. This will save you a lot of trouble.

To be a servant of the Most High in the last days will require full and complete commitment. No greater love can any person give than that they lay their life down for their friend. There is no greater friend than God, and no more glorious home than Heaven. Our choice is simple: to give what we cannot keep in order to gain what we cannot lose.

Stephen knew the heart of God on the day of his martyrdom. His picture will be played out in glorious fashion in the culminating battles for this planet. Our best word of consolation is that we should not fear, for the host of the Lord is greater by far than anything of the enemy.

As God's timetable progresses, the church will continue to experience unimaginable adjustments by the Spirit of God. The Heavenly Father will persist in revealing His purpose for the planet to the people that are partnering with Him. The ***pneumatikos*** will continue to serve the Heavenly Father in magnificent ways, and the saints will proceed from the heart of God in powerful fashion. There will be many twists and turns along the pathway of the Lord, but God will affect His purpose to the full.

Due to the climactic nature of the days that are ahead, it is imperative that the *pneumatikos* remain devoted to the heart of the Heavenly Father. Our ability to know Him, and perceive His ways will dictate our measure of usefulness and success. Like the ten virgins in the parable of Jesus, we must all take care of our lamps. The lamp represents immediate direction, and is clearly a representative sign of judging the moving of the Spirits of the Lord.[4]

Within this telling parable, we discover that the wise virgins did not triumph solely because they were in the right place at the right time. Simply living during these hours will not suffice for our victory. The telling virtue that separated wisdom from foolishness was that the lamp was operational. The *pneumatikos* must continue to function within its anointing by gleaning and knowing the purposes of God.

We cannot rely upon external sources, or appearances, in our acquisition of our marching orders. The wise virgins instructed the foolish to go elsewhere in order to obtain their oil. Undoubtedly, this had been the slumbering and impatient pattern of the foolish ones, as they were not accustomed to waiting upon Him for

---

[4] See chapter 2, section "Lamps of Fire"

themselves. The wise were ready and were inwardly equipped due to their continued practice of waiting upon the Lord.

This day, you have the opportunity to be wise or foolish, successful or a failure. The choice is up to you. God has placed you at the right place at the right time. What will you do about it? The time for the *pneumatikos* and saints is now.

When Jesus spoke of the time of the end, He focused upon the fact that we should not dwell in fear. In truth, He said that our discussion should be such that we would be able to comfort one another with our words. This is not a time for fear, as this is our greatest hour! May the Peace of the Lord Jesus Christ, the King of Saints, reign in you. Amen!!!

Pneumatikos Publishing

P.O. Box 595351
Dallas, Texas 75359
(214) 821-5290 fax (214) 821-6760
www.pneumatikos.com or email info@pneumatikos.com

BOOKS YOU NEED TO READ!!

Divers Tongues — By Ronald W. Crawford
The author, a seasoned pastor, takes us through God's Word as he unveils the strategic communication tool of divers tongues. This long hidden and misunderstood gifting brings spiritual warfare victories that are both wondrous and compelling.

The Saints — By Ronald W. Crawford
In these last days, God is mobilizing an army of mighty men to do battle with the forces of the enemy. The King of Saints is recruiting, equipping and assigning these warriors against the forces of the antichrist. The Saints are the remnant that will welcome the Kingdom of God.

Princes of the Dark Realm — By Ronald W. Crawford
Our enemy is Satan, but he does not fight alone. The Bible directly identifies many evil rulers with which the church must contend, each with very specific tactics and purposes within the kingdom of darkness. The author describes several of these beings from the vantage point of the Word of God, as well as from direct encounters with them. Let us not be ignorant of any of the devices of our enemies. (Coming Soon)

Ministering with Angels — By Paul David Harrison
One of the distinguishing characteristics of the culminating events in God's timetable will be the influx of the angelic in our churches and individual lives. They are coming at God's bidding to impart gifts and anointings reserved for these last days

Ministering from our Heavenly Seats — By Paul David Harrison
Scripture says God has "…made us sit together in heavenly places in Christ Jesus". The author describes what it is really like to pray and minister from the seats of authority God has purposed and prepared for His Son's bride, the church. (Coming Soon)

Breaking Chains of Darkness — By Charles Baker, PhD.
The author shares from both scripture and experience how demons are expelled, curses are broken and how enemy tactics that establish strongholds in Christians can be ended by the Blood of Jesus.

ORDER FORM

BOOKS	# of Books	Price Each	Total
Ministering with Angels By Paul David Harrison (Also in Spanish)		10.00	
Divers Tongues By Ronald Crawford		10.00	
Divers Tongues Self-Study Course (need book to complete)		10.00	
Ministering from our Heavenly Seats By Paul David Harrison	COMING SOON		
The Saints By Ronald Crawford		10.00	
Pneumatikos By Ronald Crawford		10.00	
Princes of the Dark Realm By Ronald Crawford	COMING SOON		
Breaking Chains of Darkness By Charles Baker, PhD.		10.00	

Please make checks payable to:

Pneumatikos Publishing
P.O. Box 595351
Dallas, Texas 75359
(214) 821-5290

Sub Total

Sales Tax 8.25%
(Texas Residents only)

Shipping

Total

Shipping
1 book — add $2.00
2 -5 books — add $3.00
6-14 books — add $5.00
15-25 books — add $7.00
26 books or more — add 6%

No COD's
No charge cards
All foreign orders please triple shipping charges

Name: _____

Street or P.O. Box: _____

City: _____ *State:* ____ *Zip Code:* ____

Country: _____

Phone Number: _____